The Schizophrenic Gospel?

A Journey to Coherency through Time, Hell, and Eternity

Nancy Davis
with **Rod Davis**

I0233703

The Schizophrenic Gospel?

A Journey to Coherency Through

Time, Hell, and Eternity

by

Nancy Davis
with Rod Davis

Complete International Standard Book Number:
978-0-9847100-3-4
ISBN/SKU: 0984710035
Library of Congress Control Number: 2016943817

20 19 18 17 16 15 14 13 12 11 10 9 8 7 6 5 4 3

Unique Ink Press

Practically Peerless

Unique Ink Press
18030 Brookhurst St #316
Fountain Valley, CA 92708

www.uniqueinkpress.com

Dedication:

To a very special person. Someone who has never stopped being a truth seeker. Someone whose greatest joy is discovering the depths of truth in God's Word. If you are that person, we gladly dedicate this book to you.

About the Author

Rod and I have been married over 35 years. So you would think I would have gotten to know my husband well by now. You would be right, but you would be wrong to assume that means we always know what the other is thinking. Our premarital life experiences taught us to see the world from polar opposite perspectives. Suffice it to say we seldom walk out of the same room together. We must make an effort to compare notes to know what the other saw. You might think that is a hindrance to a relationship, but, in retrospect, I think it was providence. By the time we have worked out a picture of what we each saw or experienced, we have a far more complete understanding.

The writing of this book is a product of a nearly twenty-year journey together. It began when I first caught glimpses of inconsistencies in my theological ideas. Maybe I should say I first began to pause long enough to focus on the implications of those ideas and the meanings of various words in different Bible translations. This caused much debate and discussion between my husband, friends, our philosophy groups, and me.

I did not begin with the intent of writing a book, nor with a complete paradigm of its contents. My husband is the gifted writer in our family, and his editing of my various treatises fostered much dialogue, research, and deliberation. So, by the time we were able to come to an agreement, rest assured we had examined the subject from every possible angle. This is not an easy way to write a book, but I think it is one of the best. Rest assured, if we agree on a topic, it has undergone a rigorous validation process. You get the benefit of our debate without having to experience the hassles. This is my first book and Rod's fourth. It was written as a memoir of my spiritual journey. The personal references and interpretations are mine.

Nancy

Contents

Introduction

I have some good news and some bad news. The good news is God loves you and has a wonderful plan for your life. The bad news is if you don't accept His offer of love in this lifetime, He is going to cast you into a fiery hell from which there is no escape. That is a schizophrenic message. It is inconsistent and contradictory, but it is the Christian gospel that many people hear, either explicitly or implicitly. It sounds like God needs to save you from Himself. This book considers the damaging effects of that message on people's attitude toward God and Christianity in addition to exposing the erroneous assumptions upon which that interpretation is based.

Contrary to that message, Scripture unequivocally reiterates that God's love is boundless and His mercy everlasting. The Apostle Peter preached about the "restoration of all things, which God has spoken by the mouth of all His holy prophets since the world began" (Acts 3:21). This book will examine the meaning of "the restoration of all things". It will illuminate the inevitable implications of God's love.

When Christians hear the word universalism, they often associate it with Unitarian Universalism. UU is a belief system espousing that its followers need not adhere to any shared creed or doctrine, but that individuals should find their own truth from whatever source of inspiration they choose. However, the Bible does not teach that we should be the determiner of our own truths or create our own paths to God. The implication of that theology places the individual in the position of being god as the ultimate authority.

There are too many logical fallacies associated with UU to address in this book. Suffice it to say, this treatise completely opposes that theology. All paths do not lead to

God; some definitely lead to destruction (Matt. 7:13-4). But are all things redeemable? Can all things be restored? We believe Christ alone is the quintessential source of truth (John 14:6). The best reflection and knowledge that we have of the Eternal Divine comes through Jesus. All other claims to truth must be examined through the foundation of Christ's teaching. The historical proofs and numerous prophetic fulfillments of His life, death and resurrection bear witness to that end. No other person or historical event parallels that of Jesus. This book will contrast some theological interpretations of Scripture in light of the foundational teachings of Christ.

Most people have been taught to filter their understanding of God's Word through two millennia of evolving theological thought, rather than through the original cultural context of its writers. We have attempted to point out and set aside the filter of contemporary theological interpretations, especially when they are contradictory or seem puzzling.

Readers are often in a better position to understand the message when it is not sifted it through added language. For example, where in Scripture is the phrase *vicarious sacrifice* found? Many in the church use that language, but the word vicarious never appears in the Bible.

Vicarious sacrifice is a phrase coined in the sixteenth century to explain that Christ's crucifixion was a substitutionary death. It is meant to explain the concept that Christ died in our place. But that is also not Scriptural language. The terms in the Bible that are used to describe Christ's sacrificial death are atonement, reconciliation, and redemption, meaning freeing or loosing.

The word *vicarious* is commonly used to describe the emotional responses people have when identifying with the experiences of others. For example, parents might vicariously experience the joys and pains of their children. People vicariously experience the emotions of characters in movies, plays, or novels. To describe Christ's atonement for us as vicarious in that sense greatly diminishes what Scripture reveals. His sacrifice has much more substance, meaning, and reality than the word vicarious implies.

The Greek word used in reference to the nature of God's love is *agapé*. It was used to describe the kind of love Christ demonstrated—self-sacrificing love. The *King James Bible* originally translated the word as *charity*. However, neither the word love nor charity captures the depth of the implications of *agapé*. The characteristics of *agapé* are described in First Corinthians 13: "Love suffers long and is kind; love does not envy; love does not parade itself, is not puffed up; does not behave rudely, does not seek its own, is not provoked, thinks no evil…" (I Cor. 13:4-5). So, this book was written for those who would portray, or who believe, God is self-aggrandizing, someone who would act in any way other than with *agapé* love to save His creation from their bondage to sin and the suffering it causes.

The writing of this book has grown out of two decades of searching the Scriptures and historical Christian thought for answers to many questions raised by different Christian denominations, as well as those raised by non-Christians and atheists. It was a collaborative effort. We have studied ancient to modern Christian writers from A to Z—from Augustine's *Confessions* to emergent literature like Donald Miller's *Blue Like Jazz*.

Much of the inspiration for this book came from the writings of the Inklings and others associated with that literary gathering. The Inklings was a literary group associated with Oxford University in the 1930s and 40s. It included C.S. Lewis, J.R.R. Tolkien, Charles Williams, Owen Barfield, and others. Additionally, many writers were indirectly associated with or influenced by that group, notably Dorothy Sayers and G.K. Chesterton.

In particular, however, we would like to acknowledge the works of George MacDonald, the progenitor of the Inklings. He has arguably been called the Father of Fantasy. His novel *Phantastes* (1857), an allegory of a person's spiritual journey as a bumbling trip through fairyland, is generally acknowledged as the first book written in the genre of modern fantasy. Without him there might never have been a *Chronicles of Narnia* or a *Lord of the Rings*. C.S. Lewis said of George MacDonald, "I have never concealed the fact that I regarded him as my master; indeed I fancy I have never written a book in which I did not quote from him". MacDonald's non fiction work *Unspoken Sermons* probably influenced the thoughts expressed in this book more than any other.

The interpretation of the Scriptures presented here most closely represents the core beliefs of most of the early church for the first five centuries. Four of the six schools of theology, during that timeframe, taught Universal Salvation, (Alexandria, Caesarea, Antioch, and Edessa), one taught annihilation, (Ephesus). Only the Latin Church of North Africa espoused unending torment. Although a proponent of the Latin Church's position, Augustine's writings indicate universal salvation was a pervasive doctrine in the early church. "There are very many [*imo quam plurimi*, sometimes translated majority] in our day, who though not denying Holy Scriptures, do not believe in endless torments", Augustine (354 – 430, *Enchiria, ad Laurent*, c. 29).

Thinking outside the norm of an individual's peer group can be challenging. But everyone would probably agree that continuing to espouse error through unexamined ideas is even more dangerous. The torture tactics of the Spanish Inquisition and the extortion of indulgences were once advocated by respected church leaders as means of facilitating salvation.

Although it is not the prevailing eschatology in Western Christian thought, the belief that the Bible teaches the restoration of all things is certainly not new. Paul wrote of Christ, "He who descended is also the One who ascended far above all the heavens, that He might fill all things" (Eph. 4:10). It has been, and is presently, accepted in many Christian cultures around the world. However, it was not within the norm of our experience. So, reconsidering some peripheral theological ideas was stretching but rewarding. We hold tight to the core doctrines of the Christian church such as salvation in Christ alone, the Trinity, and the inerrancy of Scripture.

Although the purpose of this book is not to document the complete history of Christian thought, it will chronicle the Scriptural references upon which early beliefs were based. We have incorporated many passages that have been sifted out of some contemporary theology or interpreted outside of the original context.

There are many other books that describe the evolution of early Christian thought, and we encourage readers to check them out. However, the goal of this book is to bridge theological gaps. It is meant to explore Scriptural passages that have been ignored, and incorporate them into a coherent gospel message. Our objective is to propose Scriptural answers to many questions being raised by emergent thinkers or non-Christians about contemporary Western Christian thought.

We believe the Bible, in its original content, is the inspired Word of God, and the best source for interpreting the Bible is the Bible itself. The context of a Scriptural passage and the use of the same word in other passages offer the best means of understanding the original intent of the author. We follow standard Biblical exegesis methodology, and make every attempt to clarify the meaning of Scriptural passages in their context. Our heartfelt desire is for accuracy and integrity in comprehending the Divine Revelation.

When some people read a Bible passage that seems to contradict what they have been taught, they consciously or subconsciously say to themselves, "Well, that can't mean what it says because we know it says something different elsewhere". Contradictory concepts get lost in the "check it out later" part of our brains. Martin Luther once quipped, "How soon not now becomes never".

Unless otherwise noted, all Scriptural references in this book are from the *New King James Version*. Although the writing style in the NKJV is not as contemporary as other modern translations, we appreciated the colorful language that often captured subtleties missing from some newer versions. A characteristic of the NKJV edition, published by Thomas Nelson, is that it *italicizes* words that were added to the English translation for clarification, words that were not included in the original manuscripts. We included the *italics* in those quotes because in some instances the added words changed the meaning of the original passage. So when we wanted to draw the reader's attention to certain words within a quote, we emphasized them by <u>underlining</u> rather than *italicizing*.

For us, writing this book has been a fascinating journey through God's Word. What a wonderful, life-changing experience it was to fathom the depths of the implications of perfect justice balanced with perfect love. We hope you enjoy this odyssey as much as we did.

Chapter 1

The Ethical Dilemma: Unending Torment

I would rather go to hell than believe in a self-aggrandizing, megalomaniac, wrathful God! Those words were proclaimed by an atheist in a debate I heard years ago, trying to hammer home the point that such a God is unworthy of worship. Most Christians would probably empathize with that statement. Why would anyone trust or love such a God?

That representation of God has a long history. Many religious leaders have characterized God's love rather strangely. One of the most popular sermons in American Literature is Jonathan Edwards' *Sinners in the Hands of an Angry God*. Edwards was a Puritan Congregational Pastor, and this sermon has been credited with igniting a religious revival in Colonial America, the First Great Awakening. He was a staunch defender of Calvinism, and, as result of his belief in that theology, he preached this fiery passage:

> The God that holds you over the pit of hell, much as one holds a spider, or some loathsome insect over the fire, abhors you, and is dreadfully provoked: his wrath towards you burns like fire; he looks upon you as worthy of nothing else, but to be cast into the fire; he is of purer eyes than to bear to have you in his sight; you are ten thousand times more abominable in his eyes than the most hateful venomous serpent is in ours. You have offended him infinitely more than ever a stubborn rebel did his

prince; and yet it is nothing but his hand that holds you from falling into the fire every moment.[1]

On one occasion when Edwards preached this sermon, there were reports that many in the assembly swooned or cried out with uncontrolled weeping. If we believed our eternal souls were in the hands of such a God, we might have done the same.

Jonathan Edwards is often referred to as one of the greatest American theologians. Although that sermon is his most quoted and credited with inspiring the Great Awakening, the end of that awakening is not so well known. In *Water from a Deep Well*, Gerald L. Sittser explains:

> The awakening came to an abrupt end when Edwards's uncle committed suicide, two women in a nearby town went mad and people began to exhibit wild swings of emotions, from despair to elation. Criticism soon followed. Elites from Boston charged that the awakening was the product of religious "enthusiasm" (fanaticism or extremism), not genuine—that is, rational—faith (246).

Edwards would spend the rest of his life struggling with how to identify true conversion. Perhaps this was because authentic transformation is incompatible with compulsion. Fear may achieve immediate results of compliance only to foster resentment in the end. A portrayal of God, which seems to be on par with a tyrant, would reasonably create conflicting thoughts and emotions. This book will address that frightening paradigm.

Compare the implications of Edwards' message to the words Jesus used to describe God's attitude toward us:

---

[1] www.ccel.org/ccel/edwards/sermons.sinners.html, Christian Classics Ethereal Library website

Are not five sparrows sold for two copper coins? And not one of them is forgotten before God. But the very hairs of your head are all numbered. Do not fear therefore; you are of more value than many sparrows" (Luke 12:6-7).

Can I believe Jesus? John the Baptist said of Him, "He must increase, but I *must* decrease. He who comes from above is above all. ...He who God has sent speaks the words of God..." (John 3:30, 34). The evidence of Christ's resurrection would confirm John's testimony. The words of Jesus supersede the words of any other man, including Jonathan Edwards.

Describing man as *loathsome* and *abominable in his eyes* certainly appears to be at odds with the good news (gospel) of God's redeeming love and light. The contradictory message, of a good and loving heavenly Father being so excessively punishing, haunted my childhood.

Around the age of five, I asked my mother, "What is hell, and what happens to people when they die?"

I received the traditional response, "Good people go to heaven and bad people go to hell".

"What is hell?" I inquired again, sensing her discomfort.

"A place burning with fire where God sends bad people to punish them", my mother explained.

Trying to alleviate the horror that engulfed my little heart, I asked, "How long do they have to stay there?"

"Forever".

"How long is forever?"

"Well... it never ends".

That idea instilled in me a dread and distrust of the Divine Creator. There was a possibility I might escape, but I wasn't sure, as I still had a long way to go. Nevertheless, I feared my older troubled brother, whom I loved dearly, was doomed. I was angry with God for having created me. The message of God's love and redemption became overshadowed in my life by this misconception. I could not catch sight of His love through the cloud of wrath and cruelty. I spent many childhood prayers pleading to be uncreated.

George MacDonald captured this same childhood feeling of dread about God in his novel *Alec Forbes of Howglen*. A young innocent girl, Annie, has just returned home after hearing a fire and brimstone sermon. As she walks up the dark staircase to her bedroom, she thinks, "A spiritual terror was seated on the throne of the universe, and was called God—and to whom should she pray against it? Against the nighttime darkness, a deeper darkness fell".

Could an omnipotent, omniscient, omnipresent being who created a place of unending fiery torment for the mortals He brings into being, without their choosing to be born, be trusted? If God could not be trusted, how could I be saved from Him? Is God capricious? Is He punitive to some, showing grace and mercy to others? Unresolved questions like these led me to become a professed atheist at the age of thirteen. My fear that God might in fact be a wrathful, self-aggrandizing megalomaniac led me to believe that comforting myself, even with a possible illusion, would at least give some temporary respite from the nightmare. It would be another four years before I caught a glimpse of God's love.

God is not schizophrenic, and neither is His message. However, some interpretations of Scripture certainly make it appear so. This book was written to demonstrate that the Bible presents a consistent theme throughout, even though some interpretations and doctrinal statements might imply otherwise. The Bible is the best interpreter of itself. It defines its terms quite clearly for those who are willing to study it and relate the messages to the historical culture and language in which it was written.

The writer of *Hebrews* states, "Jesus Christ *is* the same yesterday, today, and forever" (Heb. 13:8). The *Gospel of John* records that Jesus showed us the character of God in physical form:

Jesus said, "If you had known me, you would have known My Father also; and from now on you know Him and have seen Him." Philip said to Him, "Lord, show us the Father, and it is sufficient for us." Jesus said to him, "Have I been with you so long, and yet you have not known Me, Philip? He who has seen me has seen the Father" (John 14:7-9).

God is not whimsical or moody. He is not angry at one moment and loving the next. Unlike some people, He does not come home after a bad day at work and take out His frustrations on his children. God's motivation for teaching and correcting the life He brought forth in His image is love, and He administers that love with wisdom. The character and nature of the Father is what Jesus demonstrated. If you want to know who the Father is, look at Jesus (John 14:9-10).

Jesus gave us the foundation by which we can interpret all other Scripture. All renderings of theology must be consistent with the teachings of Christ, first and foremost. Matthew writes that Jesus took Peter, James, and John to a mountain, "and He [Jesus] was transfigured before them. His face shone like the sun, and His clothes became as white as the light. And behold, Moses and Elijah appeared to them, talking with Him" (Matt. 17:2-3). Immediately Peter suggested they should build three tabernacles there, and "while he was still speaking, behold, a bright cloud overshadowed them; and suddenly a voice came out of the cloud, saying, 'This is My beloved Son, in whom I am well pleased. Hear Him!'" (Matt. 17:5). Jesus revealed that God is a loving, wise, and just Father. The Son is the final authority. There is no higher source of revelation. So how did Jesus teach us to understand Divine justice?

Jesus told a parable about the wages given to workers. The landowner said, "Friend, I am doing you no wrong. Did you not agree with me for a denarius? …I wish to give to this last man the same as to you. … Is your eye evil because I am good?" (Matt. 20:13-5). Here Jesus taught justice as charity. The landowner said he was doing no wrong or injustice.

Also consider the parable of the prodigal son. The father forgave simply for the contrition the son showed. There, Jesus taught justice as forgiveness. When the older brother protested, the father accounted for his pardon by explaining that the younger brother's acts, egregious as they were, resulted from being lost and disoriented. This lesson illustrates the value of relationship and that the command to love transcends the law of retribution. Justice, as taught by Christ, had nothing to do with punishment, as is often taught in Western churches today.

In Eastern Orthodoxy, the translation of the Hebrew word for *justice* has a more complex connotation than in Western Christian thought. Greek Orthodox theologian Dr. Alexandre Kalomiros wrote on the topic of justice in an article entitled *The River of Fire*. The grammar and style marks are the author's.

> The [Greek] word DIKAIWSUNH, "justice", is a translation of the Hebraic word *tsedaka*. This word means "the divine energy which accomplishes man's salvation". It is parallel and almost synonymous to the other Hebraic word, *hesed* which means "mercy", "compassion", "love", and to the word, *emeth* which means "fidelity", "truth". This, as you see, gives a completely other dimension to what we usually conceive as justice. This is how the Church understood God's justice. This is what the Fathers of the Church taught of it.[2]

Dr. Kalomiros's description is consistent with the Jewish connotation. An article in a Jewish website illuminates the word *Tzedakah*: Charity defines the word as "...meaning righteousness, justice or fairness". The article goes on to say, "In Judaism, giving to the poor is not viewed as a generous, magnanimous act; it is simply an act of justice and

---

[2] www.orthodoxpress.org/parish/river_of_fire.htm. A reprint of *The River of Fire* presented at the 1980 Orthodox Conference in Seattle, WA.

righteousness, the performance of a duty, giving the poor their due" (www.jewfaq.org).

Contemporary Western thought tends to hold that justice and punishment are synonymous. Yet in the examples Jesus taught, justice lies in forgiveness and charity, not retribution. We are specifically taught not to return evil for evil because retribution is not justice. It serves either to satisfy vengeance or as a deterrent to unjust or unrighteous acts.

Justice is what is right or fair. It is what is happening before an injustice takes place. If I have an agreement to buy something from you, say your watch, and I pay you as agreed, I am acting justly. If you give me your watch and I do not pay you, I am behaving unjustly. Throwing me in jail does not give you justice. It does not return your watch. It may give you revenge. It may also serve as a deterrent to a lawless society. Declaring that, "justice was served" feels better because it sounds nobler than saying revenge was served, but they are not the same.

In addition, justice and mercy are not opposites; they go hand-in-hand. God does not need to abdicate justice in order to show mercy. Justice executed with mercy is just. Sometimes man's sense of justice, according to the letter of the law, without being tempered by mercy, is not just at all. *Just* simply means right or fair.

If a young child throws a ball in the house and breaks something expensive, it would be unreasonable for the parent to expect the child to replace the broken item. A good parent would discipline the child in an age appropriate manner and teach him or her not to throw the ball in the house. Reasonable parents would consider those actions fair, even though the child could not pay back the full cost that resulted from the bad behavior. Justice takes into account the offender's ability, understanding, and intent, thus incorporating a rationale for mercy and forgiveness.

So, if parents consider it justice to extract a smaller recompense for acts of disobedience by their young children, why would it not be considered justice for our Heavenly

Father to do so as well? Why do some suppose that God needs to extract infinite punishment for finite acts of defiance? People may have offended an infinite being, but they are not infinite creatures.

Many acts that would be offensive to God are committed without the offender's full comprehension of the consequences of the behavior or the totality of the offense committed. The appropriate recompense for bad behavior is not infinite suffering. Jesus commands us to judge "righteously" (John 7:24). Punishment does not "satisfy" justice. An injury is not justified or rectified through retribution. Only reconciliation can make restoration. In fact, to punish infinitely someone for finite offenses seems particularly unjust. Our own laws would deem it cruel and unusual punishment.

Conversely, it is not merciful for parents to overlook disobedience or inappropriate behavior, knowing that their children will suffer greater punishment at the hands of society in the future. It is both just and merciful to teach children proper social behavior with age-appropriate discipline. Justice and mercy are not opposites. To be just is to be merciful, and to be merciful is to be just. They go hand in hand. To correct an erring child when necessary, although it may appear wrathful to the child, is to be merciful.

Jesus commands us to love our enemies, not to return evil for evil. That is a behavior meant to make us like God (Matt. 5:44-8). How can that make us like God, if God condemns his enemies to an eternity of unending torment without the possibility of redemption? Something is wrong with that doctrine.

George MacDonald (1824 – 1905) expounded on this idea in as blunt a manner as his Victorian prose would permit:

> …the notion that a creature born imperfect, nay, born with impulses to evil not of his own generating, and which he could not help having, a creature to whom the true face of God was never presented, and by whom it never could have been seen, should be thus condemned, is

as loathsome a lie against God as could find place in the heart too undeveloped to understand what justice is, and too low to look up into the face of Jesus. It never in truth found place in any heart, though in many a pettifogging brain. There is but one thing lower than deliberately to believe such a lie, and that is to worship the God of whom it is believed (*Unspoken Sermons,* "Justice", 513).

Over a hundred years after Jonathan Edwards, MacDonald penned this passage in *Unspoken Sermons*:

Is there any gospel in telling me that God is unjust but that there is a way of deliverance from him? Show me my God unjust, and you wake in me a damnation from which no power can deliver me—least of all God Himself. It may be good news to such as are content to have a God capable of unrighteousness, if only He be on their side! ("Light", 542-3).

MacDonald eloquently argues against those who would claim it is all right for God to be unjust, so long as I am in His circle of friends. If I am on His side, I don't have a problem with that doctrine. He can predestine anyone He wants to hell, so long as I'm safe. However, if it is necessary to damn billions of souls to unending and unredeemable torment in order to demonstrate mercy to me, how is that *good*? If God loves the entire world, can that really be the case?

More importantly, the illusion that people could be filled with love, righteousness, joy, and peace, while at the same time knowing some of their loved ones were so damned, would appear to be impossible. So, some have argued that God erases people's memories regarding their lost loved ones. However, Scripture certainly does not support such an idea. In fact, it reassures we will know more not less, as Jesus told us, "For there is nothing covered that will not be revealed, nor hidden that will not be known" (Luke 12:2). Paul also affirms, "Now I know in part, but then I shall know just as I also am known" (I Cor. 13:12). He also admonishes us to judge nothing before the time because the Lord will "both bring to light the hidden things of the darkness, and will manifest the counsels of the hearts" (I Cor. 4:5). Furthermore, that concept would necessitate God deceiving us about the hopeless state of most of His creation. A deliberate deception is the same as a lie, and Scripture declares, "…it *is* impossible for God to lie" (Heb. 6:18).

Thomas Talbott expands on this incongruity in *The Inescapable Love of God*. He concludes "…if I suffer from an illusion that conceals from me the nature of God, or the true import of union with God, then I am again in no position to reject God freely" (187).

Some claim that we are too depraved to judge good and evil in reference to God. That position would certainly leave us in the dark. The apostle John declared that the gospel, which literally means good news, is "the message which we have heard from Him and declare to you, that God is light and in Him is no darkness at all" (I John 1:5).

Later in the chapter "Light" in *Unspoken Sermons* George MacDonald wrote:

> Where would the good news be if John said, "God is light, but you cannot see his light; you cannot tell, you have no notion, what light is; what God means by light is not what you mean by light; what God calls light may be horrible darkness to you, for you are of another nature from him!" Where, I say, would be the good news in that? (545).

Scripture continually reiterates that God is love and light. So, when the nature of God, according to a person's understanding, seems dark, it is not only confusing but irrational. The usual response to the apparent incongruities in the Bible about God's nature is to ignore the question. God is God, and we are not. We must defer to His Divine authority, for we are incapable of understanding Divine judgment.

However, circumventing the question raises another. If infinite torment is presumably just, why should we care about saving others from God's perfect justice? Surely our abhorrence for this idea of perpetual punishment indicates an inherent doubt about the fairness of such *justice*.

Admittedly no one can completely know the mind of God. However, Christ revealed that God is Love. Consequently, some theologians teach that whatever happens to a person must be just and loving, regardless of how it appears. Perpetual torment must be good because God allows it, and He is good. Even though something appears dark Christians are supposed to believe it really is light because they assume it to be God's will; and He is light. No wonder people are confused.

George MacDonald considered that characterization of God as evil:

> Let no one persuade you that there is in Him [God] a little darkness, because of something He has said which His creature interprets into darkness. The interpretation is the work of the enemy—a handful of tares of darkness sown in the light. Neither let your cowardly conscience receive any word as light because another calls it light, while it looks to you dark. Say either the thing is not what it seems, or God never said or did it. But of all evils, to misinterpret what God does, and then say the thing as interpreted must be right because God does it, is of the devil. Do not try to believe anything that affects you as darkness ("Light", 549).

Because unending torture looks excessively punitive and out of character, a commonly presented rationale is that God is not the One doing the tormenting, but rather the people themselves choose their own irreversible fate while on earth. But that raises other questions: Is it moral to hold in full accountability those who do not fully understand the consequences of their choices? If people are only awakened to the truth after they have been condemned to unending torment and all opportunity of choice and repentance has forever been denied them, is that justice?

The reasoning continues. By using freewill to practice sin perpetually, can some people deaden their conscience to the point of rendering them incapable of repentance? The conscience gives people knowledge, or awareness, of sin. Jesus taught that without knowledge there is no sin. He told a group of Pharisees, "If you were blind [to judgment], you would have no sin…" (John 9:41). What would be the point of abandoning people who do not know why they are suffering in torment forever? Unless it accomplishes repentance and reconciliation, it would be senseless, only serving to keep evil alive.

The question really is can our freewill trump God's will. For God is "not willing that any should perish but that all should come to repentance" (II Pet. 3:9), and He "works all things according to the counsel of His will" (Eph. 1:11). Paul wrote to Timothy that God our Savior desires, "all men to be saved and to come to the knowledge of the truth" (I Tim. 2:4). In reference to salvation Jesus said, "With God all things are possible" (Matt 19:26). To claim that man's freewill can trump God's will is to deny the words of God's own Son. That claim denies the sovereignty of God.

So how is God able to accomplish His desire without violating our freewill? Paul wrote in *Philippians*, "For it is God who works in you both to will and to do of *His* good pleasure" (Phil. 2:13). So, as a potter with a lump of clay, God molds and shapes our will every day with new information. Circumstances and maturity change our wills—what we wish for and desire. To conclude that a good God would design His children, created in His image, to be forever drawn toward that which is destructive and painful to them would be illogical. No, people are designed to long for and need His love and enlightenment. Darkness only intensifies that need. Selfish desire leads to self-deception and time is often needed to reveal the destructive nature of actions that were mistakenly believed to be good at the time.

This remolding is illustrated by a passage in *Romans* that is often used out of context to support unending damnation:

> Therefore He has mercy on whom He wills, and whom He wills, He hardens. You will say to me then, "Why does He still find fault? For who has resisted His will?" But indeed, O man, who are you to reply against God? Will the thing formed say to Him who formed *it*, "Why have you made me like this?" Does not the potter have power over the clay, from the same lump to make one vessel for honor and another for dishonor? *What* if God, wanting to show *His* [note: *His* has been added to the text] wrath and to make His power known, endured with much longsuffering the vessels of wrath prepared for destruction, and that He might make known the riches of His glory on the vessels of mercy, which He had prepared beforehand for glory? (Rom. 9:18-23).

These verses are often cited to support the doctrine that God can create men tainted by sin as vessels of wrath, judge them as if they were not, punish them with unending torment, and still remain just. For, it goes on to ask, "Who are you to reply against God?" The clay does not talk back to the potter. Consider: to arbitrarily show mercy or wrath is not supported as acting justly anywhere in Scripture. So, is the Bible inconsistent?

Without putting his passage in context, it certainly sounds like a good case for the capriciousness of God. "He has mercy on whom He wills, and whom He wills He hardens". But who or what are the vessels of wrath prepared for destruction? Notice, the phrase *vessels of wrath* means that wrath was contained within those vessels by definition. So these vessels that had wrath proceeding from them are prepared for destruction. Who or what are the vessels of mercy prepared beforehand for glory?

When Paul used the analogy of the potter and the clay, he was referring to a passage from *Jeremiah* to illustrate his intended message. His audience would have been familiar with the story.

> Then I went down to the potter's house, and there he was, making something at the wheel. And the vessel that he made of clay was marred in the hand of the potter, so he made it again into another vessel, as it seemed good to the potter to make. Then the word of the Lord came to me saying O house of Israel, cannot I do with you as this potter? (Jer. 18:3-6).

The message is that the potter *remade* the marred vessel instead of totally annihilating it. It was the same lump of clay. Cannot God do with individuals as the potter did with his clay? Cannot God remake vessels of *wrath* into vessels of *mercy*? Regarding the resurrection of the soul, Paul states, "It is sown a natural body; it is raised a spiritual body" (I Cor. 15:44). Every human body is a vessel of wrath destined for physical destruction; it is in the genetic code. But God through His compassion can remake us into vessels of mercy destined for glory. That is the intent behind God being longsuffering.

The spiritual implication of this message is a direct reference to God recreating us in Christ. Paul uses the same symbolic language, referencing our bodies, in Corinthians, "It is sown in dishonor; it is raised in glory" (I Cor. 15:43). People enter this world as physical vessels of wrath and dishonor, tainted by sin through Adam, thus destined for physical destruction. This is also part of the process through which these same vessels, the same lump of clay, have been predestined for honor and glory. "For as in Adam all die, even so in Christ shall all be made alive" (I Cor. 15:22).

There are some who disregard the *all* in that verse because it does not fit with their presuppositions. They want it to say *all of some*, *all the elect*, or *all the chosen*—so long it includes them. But the *all* who shall be made alive in Christ are the same *all* who died in Adam.

Again Paul asserts, "All have been committed to disobedience that He might have mercy on all" (Rom. 11:32). Note that the *all* that receive mercy is the same as the *all* that was committed to disobedience—everyone. Who are the vessels of mercy prepared beforehand for glory? They are the remade vessels of wrath in Jeremiah's narrative. The same *all* about whom Paul is speaking.

The argument that freewill is denied, if choice for God is by design, seems unreasonable. For at the crossroads of choice every decision is influenced by many factors, such as morality, fear, self-preservation, love, hate, desire and so on. No choice is free of influences.

No choice is free of restraints. People are certainly free to will, but they are not necessarily free to acquire, or even to successfully resist what they decide against. For example, no one can resist physical death forever. None of us willed ourselves into existence, and none of us can will ourselves out of it. One may say in spiritual childhood, if I cannot have my way, I don't will to live. But I will demonstrate that scripture teaches God works all things after His wise and loving counsel. He will mature us to realize, "in the LORD I have righteousness and strength" (Isa. 45:24).

The last enemy, which is "death", will be destroyed (I Cor. 15:26), and God will be all in all (I Cor. 15:28). No Scripture supports the position that the will of man can ultimately exceed the reach of the God who designed that will.

Jesus taught that the omniscient Creator has the heart of a loving Father. In *Hope Beyond Hell*, Gerry Beauchemin characterized how that love affects our freewill:

> What father holding his little daughter's hand while crossing a busy street would ever let it go? The more she pulls, the tighter her dad squeezes. There's no way she is going anywhere! Is God any different? The argument that a person can choose hell by rejecting God as a result of

"free" will is in effect saying a little girl has more strength than her father. God has given man a "measure" of freewill, but certainly not to the degree He would allow him or her to damn themselves forever in torment. Is God less of a parent than we are (Matt. 7:11)? We extend increasing freedom to our children as they mature. Too much too soon is disastrous. He knows just how much freedom we need for our development (37).

So, what does our Father reveal in Scripture about the torments of hell? It amazed me and may surprise you.

Chapter 2

Hell:
It May Surprise You

If you look up the word *hell* in a Bible Concordance, you will be surprised at how many times it is used. Not because it is used so often, but because it is used so seldom. Hell is quite conspicuous by its relative absence. A word count from *Young's Analytical Concordance* reveals *hell* appears only 55 times.

On the other hand, *heaven* or *heavenly* appear 725 times. The words heaven or heavenly are used about thirteen times as often as the word hell. We seem to spend much more time thinking about hell than the writers of Scripture did. My intention is not to negate its reality but to keep it in proper perspective.

Misconceptions in communication and translations kept me preoccupied with the wrong emphasis. It took my focus off the redemption message. Even worse, it skewed my concept of God's character. This chapter will define terms for hell in their Scriptural and historical contexts and examine their root meanings derived from Greek and Hebrew. These will be contrasted with interpretations in contemporary usage.

For most people, their image of hell does not come from the Bible so much as it comes from literature and the arts. Those images, in turn, originated from ancient mythology, primarily Greek. When people think of hell, they usually conjure up an image that may have been inspired by Hieronymus Bosch, Stefen Lochner, or other painters of doom. Some may imagine medieval depictions of fiery torments or torture chambers.

The ancient Greek writer Homer wrote one of the earliest descriptions of Hades in *The Odyssey*. Later, Dante would describe in great detail the horrendous tortures inflicted on sinners in *The Inferno*, the first book of *The Divine Comedy*. John Milton attempted to integrate the Christian and pagan concepts of hell in *Paradise Lost*. In our modern culture, horror movies and graphic novels frequently propagate images of hell that are meant to expand one's imagination to the extremes of pain and cruelty. All this is completely contrary to what the Word of God says about the topic.

In the Bible the word *hell* is the translation for three different words from the ancient Hebrew and Greek manuscripts. However, the original words had completely different connotations from the current characterization of hell. Modern concepts have taken on an entirely different form than was originally implied, because they have been formed from non-Biblical descriptions that have influenced theological doctrines.

The two most commonly used words in the Scriptures translated as hell are the Hebrew word *Sheol* (from the Old Testament used 31 times), and the Greek word *Hades* (from the New Testament used 10 times). Both words simply mean *the unseen state*, and they are sometimes rendered *the grave*. Paul clarifies that the unseen state is eternal. "For the things which are seen are temporary, but the things which are not seen are eternal" (II Cor. 4:18). Also, one of the Psalms of David tells us that God is in *Sheol*. If I ascend into heaven, You are there; if I make my bed in hell [*Sheol*], behold, You are there" (Psa. 139:8).

The Bible clearly states that God "is there"—in *Sheol*. God is everywhere. Several other Scriptures state or imply that hell is not out of God's reach, and they will be presented later. Paul wrote, "Yet for us there is one God, the Father, of whom are all things, and we for Him; and one Lord Jesus Christ; through whom are all things, and through whom we *live*" (I

Cor. 8:6). In his speech about the "Unknown God" to the Athenians on Mars Hill (the *Areopagus*), Paul said, "For in Him we live and move and have our being" (Acts 17:28). These Scriptures state that all of us, both our physical bodies and our eternal souls, exist in Christ.

God created all things through Christ. The Gospel of John makes that clear from the very first verse. "In the beginning was the Word, and the Word was with God, and the Word was God. He was in the beginning with God. All things were made through Him, and without Him nothing was made that was made" (John 1:1-2). A few verses later, the Scripture clarifies that the Word became incarnate in Christ. "And the Word became flesh and dwelt among us, and we beheld His glory, the glory as of the only begotten of the Father, full of grace and truth" (John 1:14).

We are introduced to the word *Hades* in reference to hell when Jesus tells us the parable of the rich man and Lazarus. This parable is quoted in its entirety because we will refer to various part of it throughout this book.

> There was a certain rich man who was clothed in purple and fine linen and fared sumptuously every day. But there was a certain beggar named Lazarus, full of sores, who was laid at his gate, desiring to be fed with the crumbs which fell from the rich man's table. Moreover the dogs came and licked his sores. So it was that the beggar died, and was carried by the angels to Abraham's bosom. The rich man also died and was buried. And being in torment in Hades [the unseen state], he lifted up his eyes and saw Abraham afar off, and Lazarus in his bosom. Then he cried and said, "Father Abraham, have mercy on me, and send Lazarus that he may dip the tip of his finger in water and cool my tongue; for I am tormented in this flame". But Abraham said, "Son, remember that in your lifetime you received your good things, and likewise Lazarus evil things; but now he is comforted and you are tormented. And besides all this, between us and you there is a great

gulf fixed, so that those who want to pass from here to you cannot, nor can those from there pass to us". Then he said, "I beg you therefore, father, that you would send him to my father's house, for I have five brothers, that he may testify to them, lest they also come to this place of torment". Abraham said to him, "They have Moses and the prophets; let them hear them". And he said, "No, father Abraham; but if one goes to them from the dead, they will repent". But he said to him, "If they do not hear Moses and the prophets, neither will they be persuaded though one rise from the dead" (Luke 16:19-31).

Interestingly, this is the only reference in Scripture to an impassable gulf separating those in the afterlife. It is universally cited by those who believe that when we die, we either go to heaven (Abraham's bosom) or hell (Hades) and that nothing can change our state after that. So, it is very important to understand accurately the meaning of this story.

There are some who claim this is not a parable, but an actual account of a real person, since Lazarus is referred to by name—something not done in other parables. However, whether this is a parable or a story makes no difference. The telling of it was to illustrate a point. People remember lessons from concrete stories better than from abstract messages.

So, what is the lesson of this story? What is the conclusion? It is that even if one were raised from the dead, there would still be some who would not be persuaded to believe (vs. 31). This is an obvious reference to the fact that even though Christ was resurrected, there are still many people who do not believe.

The gulf separating the two men is located in Hades (the unseen state). It is not a material gulf any more than heaven is literally located in the bosom of Abraham. Clearly the lesson is abstract. The gulf is more likely referencing the type of mental gulf that would exist between a rocket scientist and a preschooler. This same unseen spiritual gulf would exist between people like St. Paul and Hitler.

The great gulf between Lazarus and the rich man presents a logical analogy for the same division between spiritually minded and worldly minded people. Each of those men found his situation in the afterlife was a consequence of what he had become as a result of how he had lived. Only persons who have been transformed by the renewing of their minds (Rom. 12:2) can cross that gulf and partake with Lazarus in the quenching Holy Spirit waters that spring up into everlasting life (John 4:14). Only transformation through Christ can bridge the gulf and quench that eternal thirst. Lazarus cannot cross over it any more than I can convey calculus to an infant. The rich man cannot cross either, only Christ can.

The conclusion that the rich man's state is forever unchangeable because of the impassable gulf is not substantiated. Since the gulf is described by a present tense verb, the story does not necessarily imply that it could never be crossed at another time. All we know is that the gulf could not be crossed at that time, or at least not by one's own power. To formulate a doctrine that people can never be redeemed after death based on that Scripture, one would have to assume that the creator of the gulf Himself could not bridge it.

In addition, New Testament writers had a completely different picture of the character of God than was being taught by the religious leaders of the day. The Judeo culture of the time considered wealthy people to be favored by God. Since it was the rich man in fiery torment, the story was all the more shocking to that audience. The implied message is that judging people by their material possessions could prove a serious mistake.

The third term that is often translated hell is the Greek word *Gehenna* (11 New Testament references). This is a reference to a real place, well known to the residents of ancient Jerusalem. The name *Gehenna* was literally a contraction of the Hebrew words for Valley of Hinnom. It was a place located outside Jerusalem's walls and had previously been a place where the Canaanites had burned human sacrifices. The Israelites were using it as a place where refuse was burned in a perpetually smoldering fire.

Jesus used the word *Gehenna* as a metaphorical reference to hell, specifically when fire was involved. For example, He referred to it when He taught that sin was not just an immoral physical action, but also the abstract spiritual conditions that generate such behavior.

> You have heard that it was said to those of old, "You shall not murder, and whoever murders will be in danger of the judgment." But I say to you that whoever is angry with his brother without a cause shall be in danger of the judgment. And whoever says to his brother, "Raca!" shall be in danger of the council. But whoever says, "You fool!" shall be in danger of hell fire [*Gehenna*] (Matt. 5:21-2).

Raca was a derogatory insult, but calling someone a fool implies arrogance on the part of the speaker, a sense of superiority. There are many warnings about the pitfalls of pride in all cultures.

Later Jesus warned, "Woe to you, scribes and Pharisees, hypocrites! For you travel land and sea to win one proselyte, and when he is won, you make him twice as much a son of hell [*Gehenna*] as yourselves" (Matt. 23:15). Also, "Serpents, brood of vipers! How can you escape the condemnation of hell [*Gehenna*]?" (Matt. 23:33).

James made a metaphorical reference to *Gehenna* when he warned about controlling one's tongue. "And the tongue *is* a fire, a world of iniquity. The tongue is so set among our members that it defiles the whole body, and sets on fire the course of nature; and it is set on fire by hell [*Gehenna*]" (Jam. 3:6). James uses the *tongue* to refer to the way uncontrolled speech can spew hatred, anger, vitriol, or disrespect. It can become caustic because of the spiritual refuse dump in some souls.

So, throughout Scripture the words translated as *hell* are always used to identify either the unseen state or a metaphoric place of fiery torment. Hell is never identified as representing a specific physical location. Just as the fires of *Gehenna*, the Valley of Hinnom, consumed the refuse that was thrown into it, so the evil and darkness in our lives must be burned and utterly destroyed.

Jesus drove home this point to His disciples:

> If your hand causes you to sin, cut it off. It is better for you to enter into life maimed, rather than having two hands to go to hell, into the fire that shall never be quenched—"where their worm does not die, and the fire is not quenched" (Mark 9:43-4).

In the same way that Jesus referred to cutting off one's hand to avoid evil, He goes on to include one's foot and eye as well. Each time He repeats "where their worm does not die, and the fire is not quenched", quoting from Isaiah. "…All flesh shall come to worship before Me", says the Lord. "And they have gone forth and looked on the carcasses of the men who are transgressing [note present tense] against Me. For their worm does not die, and their fire is not quenched" (Isa. 66:23-4, YLT).

This passage is often cited as meaning that hell is a place of everlasting torment. However, the contextual interpretation of the passage does not bear that out. Note that it is the fire itself that is not quenched, and the worm itself that does not die. No duration of time is mentioned regarding an individual's suffering from it. However, God's process of destroying sin is eternal because God Himself is a consuming fire (Deut. 4:24; Heb. 12:29). The true lover of God welcomes the fire. The ones who do not yet embrace it are those who do not yet know their true self or God.

Although I do not espouse George Bernard Shaw's political ideology, William Barclay cites an interesting quote from one of the famous playwright's early works, *The*

Shewing-Up of Blanco Posnet. The title character, a disreputable horse thief, described how the act of trying to save a sick child felt like entering the purposes of God for his life. "I got the rotten feeling off me for a minute of my life; and I'll go through fire to get it off me again". (*William Barclay: A Spiritual Autobiography*, 113).

Jesus concludes His lesson explaining that, "everyone will be seasoned with fire…" (Mark 9:49). The word *seasoned* implies a method of improving the taste of something. Jesus was revealing to his disciples the meaning of the prophecy in Isaiah. So, He was telling His disciples the fire was to better them. It would correct and purify them and needed to be taken seriously.

The worm serves a similar purpose to the fire. Worms have been used medically throughout history for consuming rotting flesh. They do not eat healthy tissue, only decaying matter. So, as the fire represents purification, the worm represents consuming sin.

Fire is frequently used as a metaphor throughout the Bible. "Wickedness burns as the fire…" (Isa. 9:18). Scripture says that the trials, or hardships, of our lives test our faith by fire. Peter wrote, "In this you greatly rejoice, though now for a little while, if need be, you have been grieved by various trials, that the genuineness of your faith, being much more precious than gold that perishes, though it is tested by fire, may be found to praise, honor, and glory at the revelation of Jesus Christ" (I Pet. 1:6-7).

Paul further elaborates on this refining process:

Now if anyone builds on this foundation with gold, silver, precious stones, wood, hay, straw, each one's work will become clear; for the Day will declare it, because it will be revealed by fire; and the fire will test each one's work, of what sort it is. If anyone's work, which he has built on endures, he will receive a reward. If anyone's work is burned, he will suffer loss; but he himself will be saved, yet so as through fire, (I Cor. 3:12-5).

In this passage Paul not only clarifies that man's work will be revealed through eternal fire but also that through it men will be saved. But saved from what? It is certainly not the fire. God Himself is the consuming fire. People are saved from their sins, (Matt.1:21). The word *saved* is a translation of the Greek word *sozo*, which may also be translated *made whole* (Luke 8:48). So people are literally *made whole* or completed after missing the mark through sin; they are not whitewashed.

John the Baptist preached the same message:

> I indeed baptize you with water unto repentance, but He who is coming after me is mightier than I, whose sandals I am not worthy to carry. He will baptize you with the Holy Spirit and fire. His winnowing fan is in His hand, and He will thoroughly clean out His threshing floor, and gather His wheat into the barn; but He will burn up the chaff with unquenchable fire (Matt. 3:11-2).

A winnowing fan is one that is used to blow away the chaff or hulls from the kernels of grain. The chaff, the worthless or non-nutritious part of the grain, is burned.

In all those passages, the word fire cannot logically be taken literally. It is used as a metaphor for the process by which God redeems our lives. Scriptures are clearly talking about something that is going on spiritually, not physically. Whatever evil is in us will be consumed by God in a process that in this physical world would be like fire.

Only that which is pure—gold, silver, precious stones—will remain. God is love, and the most eloquent and poetic description of love ever written is First Corinthians 13. Referred to as the love chapter, it is one of the most quoted passages in the Bible. This is how love is described:

> Love suffers long and is kind; love does not envy; love does not parade itself, is not puffed up; does not behave rudely, does not seek its own, is not provoked, thinks no evil; does not rejoice in iniquity, but rejoices in the truth;

bears all things, believes all things, hopes all things, endures all things (I Cor. 13:4-7).

Clearly, love is not self-aggrandizing. The Greek word for love in that passage is *agapé*, connoting a love that exhibits self-sacrificing behavior. The love God has for His creation.

The logical conclusion is that the wrath of the consuming fire of God must be motivated by love. That refining fire of love will consume the disease of sin in our lives, the worthless chaff; but that which is precious in His sight will be purified, that which is made in His image.

The prophet Isaiah stresses that only the righteous can live fearlessly within the consuming fire of God.

> The sinners in Zion are afraid; fearfulness has seized the hypocrites; "Who among us shall dwell with the devouring fire? Who among us shall dwell with everlasting burnings?" He who walks righteously and speaks uprightly, he who despises the gain of oppressions, who gestures with his hands, refusing bribes, who stops his ears from hearing of bloodshed, and shuts his eyes from seeing evil... (Isa. 33:14-5).

The purpose of the fires of *Gehenna* is to purge, not to torment endlessly. Since God is love, the fires with which He burns us must be redemptive in nature. Notice that the righteous dwell with and do not fear the everlasting burnings.

Children may perceive a parent's correction as wrathful, but good decent parents, would say that they take no joy in their disciplinary actions. They punish out of love, for the child's sake. Of course, not all parents are truly loving, but God always is. So, how much more out of love must flow our discipline from God who created us in His image?

The writer of Psalms 119:75 proclaims, "...in faithfulness You have afflicted me". The most common use of the word fire throughout Scripture makes reference to its purpose of refining. However, in *Revelation* there is a description of a lake of fire that some believe serves a different purpose—purely punitive in nature. Even though the popular contemporary concept of hell is a place of unending torment, this is the only reference in Scripture that, on the surface, seems to back up that idea.

In *Revelation* John writes:

> Then the beast was captured, and with him the false prophet who worked signs in his presence, by which he deceived those who received the mark of the beast and those who worshiped his image. These two were cast alive into the lake of fire burning with brimstone [sulfur]" (Rev. 19:20).

Then at the end of the Chapter, "The devil, who deceived them, was cast into the lake of fire and brimstone where the beast and the false prophet are. And they will be tormented day and night forever and ever" (Rev. 20:10).

These Scriptures have been cited to prove God's unending and unredeemable torment of the lost. However, the only ones specifically identified who were cast into the lake of fire and tormented day and night "forever" were the beast, the false prophet, and a specific devil. I hope you are not one of them. Since *Revelation* is a metaphoric vision, the beast and the false prophet can reasonably be interpreted as images of spiritual realities, rather than as literal individuals. Also, the word *forever* is used elsewhere in Scripture as hyperbole, and the meaning and implications of that word will be addressed in the next Chapter.

In the following passage John writes about the Great White Throne Judgment:

> Then I saw a great white throne and Him who sat on it, from whose face the earth and the heaven fled away. And there was found no place for them. And I saw the dead, small and great, standing before God, and books were opened. And another book was opened which is *the Book*

of Life. And the dead were judged according to their works, by the things which were written in the books. The sea gave up the dead who were in it, and Death and Hades delivered up the dead who were in them. And they were judged, each one according to his works. Then <u>Death and Hades were cast into the lake of fire</u>. This is the second death. And anyone not found written in the Book of Life was cast into the lake of fire (Rev. 20:14-5).

We are told here the *second death* is the death of Death itself and Hades. Most Bible commentators interpret the first death as being in Adam, as a result of disobeying God—original sin. But the second death is not the physical or spiritual death of people resulting from Adam's transgression. It is the death of Death itself. "The last enemy that will be destroyed is death" (I Cor. 15:24-6).

Throughout Scripture, death is referred to as separation—spiritual separation from God. So, examine again what the Scriptural reference just quoted reveals about death. First, the passage from *Revelation* states that Death and Hades delivered up the dead for judgment. Death and Hades are not souls. Secondly, after the dead were delivered up from Death and Hades, they were judged according to their works and what was written in the books. Then Death (separation from God) and Hades (the unseen state) were cast into the Lake of Fire. That would represent the end of death, that is, the end of separation from God and the end of the unseen state. All souls must now dwell with the consuming fire of God Himself, including those not written in the Book of Life.

The nature of God's love and truth illuminates and burns darkness and evil. The prophet Isaiah refers to a time "when the Lord has washed away the filth of the daughters of Zion…by the spirit of judgment and by the spirit of burning" (Isa. 4:4). The earlier reference from Isaiah (Isa. 33:14-5) described that only the righteous can dwell fearlessly in the everlasting burnings. Titus, a highly regarded Bishop around 364 A.D. wrote:

And the punishments are holy, as they are remedial and salutary in their effect on transgressions; for they are inflicted, not to preserve them in their wickedness, but to make them cease from their wickedness".[3]

Hades too was cast into the Lake of Fire. So ends the unseen state. Now, nothing is hidden, and all things are revealed. Jesus said, "For there is nothing covered that will not be revealed, nor hidden that will not be known" (Luke 12:2). Or, as Paul wrote, "For now we see in a mirror, dimly, but then face to face. Now I know in part, but then I shall know just as I also am known" (I Cor. 13:12). The Great White Throne Judgment is not a reference to the souls of people entering unending torment. Death, Hades, and sin are the things that the consuming fire of God annihilates. Truth and light annihilate lies and darkness.

The consuming fire of God does not serve as a legal compensation of an eye for an eye, which is a means of punishment or revenge. The consuming fire of God consumes that which is antithetical to God. It cleanses us from our leanings toward a destructive selfish nature. The essence of our being is transformed in it. God's revelatory truth and light will illuminate or burn, and there is no escape. As Death and Hades are annihilated, sin itself must also burn and die. Additionally, there are no references to a final judgment in Scripture. There are ample references to different judgments, but not even the Great White Throne Judgment is specifically defined as final. This is assumed because it is the last recorded judgment. But the passage in *Revelation* immediately following that judgment describes a new heaven and a new earth, and the end of former things. (More about that will be presented in Chapter 4.)

However, it is worth noting that the gates of the New Jerusalem, the place being described, are never shut. "Its gates

---

[3] From *Against the Manicheans*, quoted in *Ancient History of Universalism* by Hosea Ballou, 159.

shall not be shut at all by day (there shall be no night there)"
(Rev. 21:25). This seems to imply that there are others who
may still enter in. Why else would the doors of heaven always
be open? Scripture goes on to explain that nothing that defiles
it can enter, but anyone who has been purified certainly can.

In the last chapter of the last book of the Bible we are
told, "Blessed are those who do [not did] His commandment,
that they may have the right to the tree of life, and may enter
through the gates into the city" (Rev. 22:14). "And the Spirit
and the bride say, 'Come!' And let him who hears say,
'Come!' And let him who thirsts come. Whoever desires, let
him take the water of life freely" (Rev. 22:17).

Who beckons the thirsty to come and partake of the water
of life? The Holy Spirit and the bride of Christ, the church.
Who do they offer this water to? *Whoever desires.* The verse
does not say only the elect, chosen, or saved may drink. The
invitation is to whoever desires, and this living water is the
Holy Spirit of God given through Jesus Christ (John 7:37-9).

Of course, not all who are offered water will drink it; and
many who refuse will be cast into outer darkness. In the
Parable of the Wedding Feast, Jesus described outer darkness
as the place for those people who were invited to the wedding
feast but did not come clothed in wedding garments.

> The kingdom of heaven is like a certain king who
> arranged a marriage for his son, and sent out his servants
> to call those who were invited to the wedding; and they
> were not willing to come. Again, he sent out other
> servants, saying "Tell those who are invited, 'See, I have
> prepared my dinner; my oxen and fatted cattle are killed,
> and all things *are* ready. Come to the wedding.'" But they
> made light of it and went their ways, one to his own farm,
> and another to his business. And the rest seized his
> servants treated *them* spitefully, and killed *them.* But
> when the king heard *about it,* he was furious. And he sent
> out his armies, destroyed those murderers, and burned up
> their city. Then he said to his servants, "The wedding is

ready, but those who were invited were not worthy. Therefore go into the highways, and as many as you find, invite to the wedding". So those servants went out into the highways and gathered together all whom they found, both bad and good. And the wedding *hall* was filled with guests. But when the king came in to see the guests, he saw a man there who did not have on a wedding garment. So he said to him, "Friend, how did you come in here without a wedding garment?" And he was speechless. Then the king said to the servants, "Bind him hand and foot, take him away and cast *him* into outer darkness; there will be weeping and gnashing of teeth". For many are called, but few are chosen, (Matt. 22:2-14).

This parable is one of three references to outer darkness. It refers to the kingdom of heaven as a wedding feast where those invited don't show up and at least one who does is not properly dressed. Those who initially refused to come symbolize some of the Jews, specifically the religious leaders and their followers. They were the ones who "seized his servants, treated them spitefully, and killed them". Stephen, the first martyr for Christ, bears out this understanding when he exclaimed at his trial before the Sanhedrin:

You stiff-necked and uncircumcised in heart and ears! You always resist the Holy Spirit; as your fathers did, so do you. Which of the prophets did your fathers not persecute? And they killed those who foretold the coming of the Just One, of whom you now have become the betrayers and murderers... (Acts 7:51-2).

In 70 A.D. the members of the Sanhedrin residing in Jerusalem were killed, and the city was burned.

With that rejection of the Messiah, everyone else was invited to the wedding feast. Paul wrote to the Romans, "...*even* us, whom he called, not of the Jews, only, but also of the Gentiles" (Rom. 9:24). However, one must come properly dressed for the feast, in the righteousness of Jesus.

This interpretation is further clarified when one realizes Jesus' parable was a reference to the prophet Zephaniah.

> The day of the LORD *is* at hand, for the LORD has prepared a sacrifice; he has invited His guests. And it shall be in the day of the LORD's sacrifice, that I will punish the princes and the king's children, and all such as are clothed with foreign apparel" (Zeph. 1:7-8).

The sacrifice is, of course, Jesus Himself.

Jesus said, "I am the light of the world. He who follows Me shall not walk in darkness, but has the light of life" (John 8:12). Since Jesus is our light, those who are not clothed in the illumination of His righteousness necessarily dwell in darkness. The consequence of living in darkness, refusing the light of Christ, will be pain and suffering. Each time Jesus referred to outer darkness it is followed by the phrase *weeping and gnashing of teeth*. So, such a place should not be taken lightly. Jesus came into the world to save us from that fate.

However, note that outer darkness is not described as a place from which there is no possibility of redemption. The darkness is designed and bound to intensify the thirst for light. The invitation to drink of the water of life is still freely offered to whoever desires.

The apocalyptic visions of the last book in the Bible, *The Revelation*, generates a great deal of controversy. Although some in the church take it literally, most of the language is obviously metaphoric, like a dream. It is, after all, a vision that Christ gave to John of things that "must shortly take place" (Rev. 1:1). Because the book is a vision, it would be unwise to take a single reference from it, especially one that is not confirmed elsewhere in Scripture, as a source for foundational doctrine. When a literally rendered explanation of a passage is contradicted frequently elsewhere in Scripture, it should be understood as symbolic.

The fact that Death and Hades are cast into the lake of fire points to the end of death and hell. There is no longer separation from God (death), and there is no longer an unseen state (hell). Besides John's reference in *Revelation*, Paul describes the end of death as follows:

> Then *comes* the end, when He delivers the kingdom to God the Father, when He puts an end to all rule and all authority and power. For He must reign till He has put all enemies under His feet (I Cor. 15:24-5).

Who or what are these enemies? They are the things that seek rule, authority and power that He will put an end to, such as pride, jealousy, hatred, greed, lust, and so on. "The last enemy that will be destroyed is death" (I Cor. 15:24-6). These enemies of love, that kill, will be destroyed, thus destroying death itself. It appears that the lake of fire is once again the consuming or refining fire of God's love, the same as it has been throughout the rest of Scripture.

References to the eternal nature of the fire have fostered a continuing attempt to justify unending torment. Some Theologians assert the nature of sin against an infinite God is infinite, and therefore never ending punishment is justified. Such rationalization unfortunately springs from the confusion of mistaking punishment for justice as discussed in Chapter 1.

Still, the logic of that argument fails when examined on infinite (past and future) time presuppositions. Being finite, people could only pay the penalty for their sins into the infinite future. Therefore, the infinite past would remain unpunished. Since God is infinite past and future, there is no retribution that would equate to the nature of an offense against God. This renders complete repayment or perfect justice impossible to achieve.

Thus, the emphasis on the necessity of infinite punishment to satisfy God's immutable justice raises a question about the meaning of Christ's sacrifice. The theological obsession over extracting retribution would seem to demand that Christ be infinitely punished for our sins. This is an absurd presupposition. We know that Christ has ceased to suffer.

This concept of infinite past and infinite future assumes that eternity can be expressed as a timeline with no beginning and no ending. However, that is not what the Scriptures teach about eternity. The concept of eternity cannot be subjected to such a simple and finite limitation.

Chapter 3

Eternity:
Not a Very Long Time

This chapter holds the key to understanding the meaning of many Scriptural passages cited throughout this book. So it is important to present the concept of eternity as clearly as possible, since the misconception of this term frequently seems to be a source of supposed contradictions or theological confusion. The main point of this chapter is that eternity cannot be summarized as endless time. It is not a very, very long time. It is not time. It may be a state to which time has no application. Eternity goes beyond the range of what we generally refer to as the fourth dimension.

Scriptural references to eternity allude to a concept that transcends the fourth dimension. Paul wrote to Titus, "...in hope of eternal life which God, who cannot lie, promised before time began..." (Tit. 1:2). The Greek phrase translated *time* in *The New King James* version is translated *the world* in the *King James Bible*. The reason why the same Greek words are rendered differently is that the phrase literally translates *before the times of the ages*. That would imply before the world and the fourth dimension began.

Imagining time as a numerical sequence, which may be extended endlessly, is a different concept from the Scriptural use of the word eternal. As it relates to the concept of infinity, time has been presented as an unending series of events. That which is infinite will never cease. However, the dictionary definition of eternal is something that exists outside of, or beyond, time. So, by the dictionary definition as well as by Scriptural exegesis, eternity transcends an age, such as the one in which the world exists.

The Greek word that is usually translated eternal or everlasting is *aionios*, the root of our English word eon (or aeon). The literal translation of *aionios* is simply *age-lasting*. The noun *aion* becomes an adjective when the suffix *–ios* is added. Thus, *age* becomes *age-lasting*. Its connotation is of indefinite (not infinite) duration. Because *aionios* has been used to describe God Himself (Heb. 9:14), some assume it must mean unending, since that is the nature of God. However, God existed before "the time of the ages" (Tit. 1:2). So He is not only age lasting, but He transcends *aionios*, times and ages.

There is also one other Greek word translated *eternal* and *everlasting* that should be addressed—*aidios*. Its meaning is more obscure. It is formed from *a-*, meaning no or negative, and *-idios*, meaning one's own or private world, as opposed to *kosmos*, meaning a shared or perceived world. Thus it literally means not perceived. It is equivalent to the word *hades*, where *Ha-* (like *a-*) is a negative, and *-des* (like *–idios*) means to see. So, both *aidios* and *hades* literally mean the same thing: *imperceptible* or *an unseen state*. *Strong's Concordance* translates *aidios* as *everduring* (forward and backward).

There are only two Scriptures that use that word. Romans 1:20 states, "For since the creation of the world His invisible *attributes* are clearly seen, being understood by the things that are made, *even* His eternal power and Godhead, so that they are without excuse". Even God's imperceptible power can be clearly understood through His creation. The context of this passage is about perception so "the unseen state" seems to be the relevant interpretation.

Jude verse 6 states, "And the angels who did not keep their proper domain, but left their own abode, He has reserved in everlasting chains under darkness for the judgment of the great day". This verse implies there are fallen angels who are being kept in unseen chains of darkness waiting for the judgment day. The translation everlasting certainly becomes moot in a context of waiting for a definitive day of judgment. Again, imperceptible would be the relevant translation.

From a person's position in linear time, trying to comprehend eternity is like a point on a line segment trying to observe the shape of something outside its bounds. A point that is connected to other points on the line can, in a sense, experientially comprehend what it is connected to. However, if the point on the line segment is surrounded by a square, engulfed by a cube, or enmeshed within a multidimensional polyhedron, the point, being connected only to the line segment, will never be able to visualize experientially the shape of what is beyond. The point may be able to comprehend that something lies outside its ability to perceive, but a point can never physically know the shape of the eternal. The mathematics of this concept was first presented in an 1884 classic novella *Flatland: A Romance of Many Dimensions by* Edwin Abbott.

Scripture gives us some ideas to help understand eternity, but without a doubt we see through a glass darkly. Paul tells us that eternal things are not seen. "For our light affliction, which is but for a moment, is working for us a far more exceeding and eternal weight of glory, while we do not look at the things which are seen, but at the things which are not seen. For the things which are seen are temporary, but the things which are not seen are eternal" (II Cor. 4:17-8). *Eternal* is not described as an unending series of events. This Scripture implies that what we are doing in the temporal realm is working for us in an unseen manner in an eternal realm.

Certainly temporal events, Paul's allusion to "our light affliction", are working to accomplish something beyond the bounds of time, an "eternal weight of glory". Perhaps the eternal is playing out in the temporal, while the temporal changes the eternal. However, since we are not going to be able to know exactly what that means until we have transcended the bounds of time, it would be best for now to stick to what we can understand. So this chapter will focus only on how the Scriptures describe and define eternity.

Jesus said, "And this is eternal life, that they may know You, the only true God, and Jesus Christ whom You have sent" (John 17:3). Eternal life is to know God! It is interesting that the word "time" does not appear in Christ's description of eternal life. When Jesus spoke those words He was apparently clarifying the misconception that eternal life was a time continuum. From His point of view, eternal life was a life-giving force, a personal relationship with God. This would also imply that eternal damnation would be the antithesis, not to know God experientially either in this realm or the next.

William Barclay, a well-respected theologian whose books are standard reference sources for many Protestant pastors, goes into much more detail on the enigmatic nature of *aionios* in his classic *New Testament Words*. This is how he concluded his study:

> We shall never enter into the full ideas of eternal life until we rid ourselves of the almost instinctive assumption that eternal life means primarily life which goes for ever…. Life is only of value when it is nothing less than the life of God—and that is the meaning of eternal life (41).

It was probably that understanding of eternal as being an attribute of God and not an endless period of time that influenced Barclay to profess universal reconciliation. In *A Spiritual Autobiography*, he wrote, "But in one thing I would go beyond strict orthodoxy—I am a convinced Universalist. I believe that in the end all men will be gathered into the love of God" (58).

Our comprehension of eternity must necessarily be abstract. Trying to understand eternal realities through physics is as impossible as a person born blind trying to understand color. Blind people can only relate to the concept of color by comparing it to something else they can experience. Thus, saying that red is hot and blue is cold does not really help the blind to comprehend color as such. However, it gives them a way to relate to color in an experiential manner.

Although using physical analogies as metaphors for spiritual ones offers only a limited representation, it is the way Jesus taught us to visualize the unseen realm. He spoke in parables so that we could relate to spiritual truths in some frame of physical reference. After Jesus told His disciples the parable of the sower:

> Then His disciples asked Him, saying, "What does this parable mean?" And He said, "To you it has been given to know the mysteries of the kingdom of God, but to the rest it is given in parables…" (Luke 8:9-10).

To those who do not experience the transcendent spirit of God dwelling in them, the parables must be a mystery.

Following that example, a modern metaphor for eternal life might be our dependence upon oxygen. That element is a necessary life-giving force. It is fuel producing the energy we need to maintain viability. Loss of ability to carry oxygen through the bloodstream results in illness and death. Years ago a serious bout of bacterial pneumonia left me starving for that unseen essential. It made even small exertions, such as rolling over in bed, difficult and painful. I was dying and longed for the health and energy only oxygen could provide.

An oxygen atom will exist in its atomic form as long as it is oxygen. Unless the atom undergoes a thermonuclear reaction, it will remain the same. It may change physical forms, such as by bonding with two hydrogen atoms to form a molecule of water, but the individual atom remains the same. I remember when I was a child hearing that we have all breathed some of the same oxygen atoms that were breathed by Julius Caesar. I doubt that is a statement scientifically provable. It does not sound like a postulate that could be proven through the rigors of the scientific method. However, the principle is that within our frame of reference an oxygen atom, or any other atom for that matter, exists unchanged forever in an unseen state to us. Eternal life is oxygen for our souls.

The Apostle John describes another time when Jesus made a distinction between eternal life and time.

> Jesus walked in the temple, in Solomon's porch. Then the Jews surrounded Him and said to Him, "How long do You keep us in doubt? If You are the Christ, tell us plainly". Jesus answered them, "I told you, and you do not believe. The works that I do in My Father's name, they bear witness of Me. But you do not believe, because you are not My sheep, as I said to you. My sheep hear My voice, and I know them, and they follow Me. And I give them eternal life, and they shall never perish; neither shall anyone snatch them out of My Father's hand" (John 10:23-8).

The statement "I give them eternal life, and they shall never perish" would be redundant if eternal life was the same as unending time. The *and* divides the two realms of life and time. To know the Father is eternal life, while existing forever is a separate matter. Theoretically, one could exist forever without knowing the Father.

Importantly, Scripture does not place any time limit on when Jesus could provide eternal life. Could it be given in *Sheol* (hell) after physical death? If there was a time limitation needed to receive a gift that would save one from unending torment, it would seem a significant prerequisite that it would have been clearly stated somewhere. But none of the Scriptures ever specify that restriction. In fact, some passages referencing the dead suggest otherwise.

What do the Scriptures say about eternal damnation? The *Epistle of Jude* mentions suffering from eternal fire.

> …As Sodom and Gomorrah, and the cities around them in similar manner to these, having given themselves over to sexual immorality and gone after strange flesh, are set

forth as an example, suffering the vengeance of eternal fire (Jude 7).

Note that the fire is described as eternal, but not the duration of the suffering from it, as was explained in the previous chapter.

Certainly it would be better to receive the gift of eternal life in this realm rather than the next. Clearly we cannot fathom the full consequences of not doing so; and there are numerous warnings that imply the peril of rejection. Jesus said, "...For if you do not believe that I am, you will die in your sins" (John 8:24). All the same, He did not say that God was powerless to save those who had passed over.

Why else would Jesus preach to spirits in prison who had died in the days of Noah? This is referenced by Peter:

> For Christ also suffered once for sins, the just for the unjust, that He might bring us to God, being put to death in the flesh but made alive by the Spirit, by whom also He went and preached to the spirits in prison, who formerly were disobedient, when once the Divine longsuffering waited in the days of Noah, while the ark was being prepared, in which a few, that is, eight souls, were saved through water (I Pet. 3:18-20).

That passage states that Christ preached to the spirits of those who had died at the time of Noah. Peter goes on to clarify:

> They will give an account to Him who is ready to judge the living and the dead. For this reason the gospel was preached also to those who are dead, that they might be judged according to men in the flesh, but live according to God in the spirit (I Pet. 4:5-6).

The *New International Version* (NIV) translation of that passage reads, "the gospel was preached to those who are *now* dead". A footnote explains: "This preaching was a past event.

The word 'now' does not occur in the Greek, but it is necessary to make it clear that the preaching was done, not after these people had died, but while they were still alive". The word *now* was added to clarify the translators' doctrinal position, and since adding a word seemed insufficient, they added a footnote to explain their interpretation.

Other commentators interpret the passage as meaning that Noah, not Christ, preached to those who were living during the time before the flood. All of them are *now* dead. No wonder this passage is frequently referred to as one of the most difficult to understand in all Scripture. If people have to make it mean something it does not say because they don't agree with it, it must, indeed, be the most difficult of passages.

Christ did not preach to "the spirits in prison" until after He was "put to death in the flesh but made alive by the Spirit", and the time of His crucifixion has been estimated to be about three thousand years after the flood. So, Christ was preaching to people who had been dead for a very long time. Peter plainly states that Christ preached after His death, to "spirits... who formerly were disobedient" and had lived during "the days of Noah".

Some, troubled by the former renderings, have claimed we don't know what Christ's message was, and that it might not have been a message of salvation. That would make one wonder what He was preaching. It has been suggested that Christ went to announce to those dead spirits that He died to save the world, but that it was too late for them. Such a message sounds cruel, certainly not consistent with the loving nature Christ demonstrated throughout the gospels.

What we know of the character of Christ makes it difficult to believe that He descended into hell to preach what that interpretation implies: "I have come here to thank you for being examples of those who are without hope, those who have passed beyond My reach or mercy. You make those who are saved feel much better, knowing they have escaped your fate". Such speculation is, of course, ridiculous.

Peter clarifies exactly what Christ preached: "the gospel was preached to those who are dead, that they might …live according to God in the spirit". The reason for the preaching was to redeem those lost souls. Christ was preaching to them that they might live. Isaiah 55:11 states, "So shall My word be that goes forth from My mouth; it shall not return to Me void, but it shall accomplish what I please, and it shall prosper *in the thing* for which I sent it". Christ, the "Word" of God sent forth, will accomplish the salvation of those imprisoned souls who were disobedient in the days of Noah.

What we know about Peter from the gospels is that he was a person who said whatever he was thinking, often to his own detriment. Rightly or wrongly, everyone always knew where Peter stood. It is unlikely that Peter changed into someone who would communicate in an academic or esoteric style. That is not the type of person he was. The best interpretation of Peter's writing would be the most straightforward one, for that would be consistent with the type of person Scripture revealed him to be. Peter was the prototypical person who was always thinking out loud. He spoke his mind. He said what he meant, and he meant what he said.

The word eternal indicates an unseen state that cannot be completely understood from our perspective. However, does the translation "forever" imply an infinite time continuum? Similar to *eternal*, most words translated as "ever", like *aionios*, denote *age-lasting*. Frequently, the word is used as hyperbole, an exaggeration intended to stress a point or communicate some unknown quantity.

We often overemphasize descriptions for dramatic effect. "That lecture dragged on *forever*", or, "I thought it would *never end*". Such expressions are obviously not meant to be taken literally. The writers of Scripture frequently used figurative language, as do most writers.

The prophet Isaiah described the destruction of the city of Edom as follows:

For My sword shall be bathed in heaven; indeed it shall come down on Edom and on the people of My curse, for judgment…. Its land shall become burning pitch. It shall not be quenched night and day; its smoke shall ascend forever. From generation to generation it shall lie waste; no one shall pass through it forever and ever (Isa. 34:5, 9-10).

Ancient Edom is not still burning. There is no place on earth where smoke has been and will be continuously rising forever and ever. The passage is either referring to smoke in a figurative sense, or the prophet is using hyperbole.

The same terminology of smoke rising forever is used metaphorically in *Revelation* to describe the fall of the Great Harlot, Mystery Babylon. "Again they said, 'Alleluia!' Her smoke rises up forever and ever!" (Rev. 19:3). New Testament writers commonly used Old Testament expressions as metaphors and symbolic references that would be understood within the cultural context of the day. Like Edom, Mystery Babylon will be judged and the smoke (remaining vapor) will not be forgotten.

The use of hyperbole is not limited to the unlimited. It can also be applied to expressions of large numbers. For example, the Psalmist writes, "For every beast of the forest *is* Mine, *and* the cattle on a thousand hills" (Psa. 50:10). Does that mean the cattle on hill number 1001 and those beyond are not His? The "thousand hills" in that passage is figurative, not literal. The passage unequivocally means that all creatures are His.

About the "land of My people", the prophet Isaiah wrote:

Because the palaces will be forsaken, the bustling city will be deserted. The forts and towers will become lairs forever, a joy of wild donkeys, a pasture of flocks—until the Spirit is poured upon us from on high, and the wilderness becomes a fruitful field, and the fruitful field is counted as a forest (Isa. 32:14-5).

Isaiah specified that forever is not literally an endless length of time. The desolation of the land will last "until the Spirit is poured upon us".

The prophet Jeremiah wrote:

And you, even yourself, shall let go of your heritage which I gave you; and I will cause you to serve your enemies in the land which you do not know; for you have kindled a fire in My anger which shall burn forever" (Jer. 17:4).

Yet in Isaiah we read, "For I will not contend forever, nor will I always be angry; for the spirit would fail before Me, and the souls *which* I have made" (Isa. 57:16).

Different people wrote these prophecies at varying times, but they are both about the same people, the Israelites. The fact that one says, "My anger will burn forever" and the other, "I will not contend forever, nor will I always be angry illustrates that forever is used figuratively, not literally.

However, even if a literal interpretation of the word *forever* is assumed, there is no direct reference in Scripture to people being tormented in hell forever and ever. There is one verse in *Revelation* that mentions unending torment referred to in the last chapter, "The devil, which deceived them, was cast into the lake of fire and brimstone where the beast and the false prophet are. They will be tormented day and night forever and ever" (Rev. 20:10). Again, there are only three beings or entities that will be tormented forever and ever: the devil, the beast, and the false prophet. Note there is only one specific devil included.

By trying to analyze eternal life, death, and time from isolated passages in the Bible, one may miss the meaning and purpose of the complete message. A scientist attempting to logically analyze and quantify the beauty of a rose, might approach the problem by systematically separating the flower into its component parts. The net result could be a symmetrical arrangement of petals and stems, pistols and stamen. But where is the beauty of the rose? Where is the truth of its reason for existence?

Ethereal glory cannot be discovered through the scientific method. The meaning lies in the reason God formed the individual parts into the whole. The meaning lies in its transcendent beauty imparted to the viewer. George MacDonald wrote:

> The truth of a thing, then, is the blossom of it, the thing it is made for. Truth in a man's imagination is the power to recognize this truth of a thing. Wherever, in anything that God has made, in the glory of it, be it sky or flower or human face, we see the glory of God, there a true imagination is beholding a truth of God. And now we must advance to a yet higher plane (*Creation in Christ*, 146).

So, to calculate the worth of something by adding up the value of its individual components is simply amiss. The rose loses the truth of its beauty when half of the rose is missing. Many years ago there was a study published that calculated the worth of a human body at about $1.98. That amount was based on the current market value of the chemical elements that make up the average sized body, if they were isolated. People were shocked that life was so cheap. For several years following that study the calculation would be updated to reflect changing market values. That way people could feel the value of their life was improving through inflation.

It is clear that $1.98 was and is a meaningless measure for the value of life. As one blogger put it, using that standard for determining worth would mean that the value of the Mona Lisa would be about $0.24. The real worth of anything is determined not by the cost of its components, but by the significance others assign to its assembled parts. Otherwise a $1000 bill would be worth the same amount as $1 bill, about ten cents. Just as the reason for the rose is found in the totality of the rose, the value of life is found in the completed eternal objective of creation.

Paul wrote to the *Ephesians*:

> Having made known to us the mystery of His will, according to His good pleasure which He purposed in Himself, that in the dispensation of the fullness of the times He might gather together in one all things in Christ, both which are in heaven and which are on earth-in Him (Eph. 1:9-10).

This unification and gathering is the blossom of life. God will not abandon His ultimate purpose. He will recover all His lost sheep because there are no expendables in Love's economy. What caring parent would consider a child nonessential to the family?

The beauty of God's message about eternal life is found in the whole of Scripture, not the individual components. The love, the discipline, the unity, and the universal gathering of all things in Christ complete the picture. Paul drives the point home beautifully, "The last enemy *that* will be destroyed is death" (I Cor. 15:26). Remember, He is the "Savior of all men" (I Tim. 4:10). If only some get saved that makes Him the Savior of only some.

To summarize, eternity is a spiritual concept, not a time continuum. Eternal life is a life-giving force in and of itself, like oxygen is for our bodies. The Scripture says that eternal life is to know God. Through that experience, we access the life energy of love, joy, and peace. If people are not connected to a spiritual life-sustaining source, they will die. They will cease to experience the life-giving force of God's love. World history testifies to that reality. But can they be resurrected and restored?

Just as a branch must be bound to its life source to live, so we must be bound to our source of eternal life in Christ. Jesus said:

I am the vine, you are the branches. He who abides in Me, and I in him, bears much fruit; for without Me you can do nothing. If anyone does not abide in Me, he is cast out as a branch and is withered…" (John 15:56).

But the spiritually withered are not without hope. Jesus said, "…the one who comes to Me I will by no means cast out" (John 6:37). His arms are always open.

The antithesis of eternal life is eternal damnation, which is the absence of that life-giving force of God's love through Christ the spiritual vine. That which is separated from God, is left to endure the consequences of a fragmented dying nature. We are designed to need connectedness in a manner that transcends the physical. Can we really believe God will forsake His great design? Will He really give up and abandon His work to incomplete worthlessness?

Significance can only be realized in that which transcends the temporal since the material will cease to exist. It is, in fact, ceasing to exist at this very moment as physical cells are dying and changing in every individual. Connection with the eternal love gives rise to the only lasting significance.

Christ is our connection, and before the culmination, He will "put an end to all rule and all authority and power" (I Cor. 15:24). This is the nature of the kingdom He will deliver to the Father. All our claims to godhood will be replaced with brotherhood. Esteeming the egos of men and earthly powers will be revealed one day as meaningless in their temporality. Only that which has incorporated the character of God can withstand His presence. And what is that character? Love, the most powerful force in the universe.

In *Matthew*, Christ rebukes the citizens of some cities where He had performed "mighty works" but the people refused to believe in His message of love. They continued in their evil. Needless to say, this is not one of Christ's most popularly quoted passages. He declared:

Woe to you, Chorazin! Woe to you, Bethsaida! For if the mighty works which were done in you had been done in Tyre and Sidon, they would have repented long ago in sackcloth and ashes. But I say to you, it will be more tolerable for Tyre and Sidon in the day of judgment than for you. And you, Capernaum, who are exalted to heaven, will be brought down to Hades; for if the mighty works which were done in you had been done in Sodom, it would have remained until this day. But I say to you that it shall be more tolerable for the land of Sodom in the day of judgment than for you (Matt. 11:21-4).

The words of Christ in that passage focus one's attention on the plight of the people in those cities that saw His miracles firsthand yet still refused to believe.

However, Loyal F. Hurley in a booklet entitled *The Outcome of Infinite Grace* considered the implication of Christ's statements on the cities of Tyre, Sidon, and Sodom, rather than on the cities where Jesus walked, Chorazin, Bethsaida, and Capernaum. He wrote:

Jesus... said that if Tyre and Sidon had only witnessed the mighty works which were done in Chorazin and Bethsaida they would have repented long ago in sackcloth and ashes. That is, more knowledge and information would have brought them to repentance. Do you think, therefore, that God will torment the inhabitants of Tyre and Sidon forever because of their lack of knowledge? Again, He said that if Sodom could have witnessed the mighty works that were done in Capernaum "it would have remained until this day". Do you think that the inhabitants of Sodom will be tormented forever just because they lacked the opportunities of Capernaum? Nay, indeed! God will not inflict ultimate punishment on men who have not had ultimate knowledge. "For this is good and acceptable in the sight of God our Savior; Who will have all men to be saved, and to come unto the knowledge of the truth" (I Tim.2:3, 4). It is not just a matter of one "chance" (pp. 42-3).

To conclude that the inhabitants of those cities are forever damned as a result of God's deliberately withholding information that He knew would bring about their repentance is to conclude that God is neither good nor loving, contrary to what Scripture reveals throughout.

Critics label this idea of universal reconciliation a "second chance" gospel. People don't need to worry if they reject God in this life, because they will get another chance after they are dead. Hurley answers:

> ...people say that Reconciliation makes a "second chance" gospel. No, no, no! We do not have a "first chance" gospel, nor a "second chance" gospel. Salvation is not by "chance," it is by grace! Infinite grace! (41).

Most of us did not profess belief in the gospel the first time we heard it. Many of us had innumerable chances to accept God's calls for reconciliation in our lives before His love finally won us over. Salvation is not a matter of chance; it is the outcome of infinite, amazing grace.

However, death and hell should be a little more worried. "Then Death and Hades were cast into the lake of fire" (Rev. 20:14). Following the death of Death and Hades, "Then I, John, saw the holy city, New Jerusalem, coming down out of heaven from God, prepared as a bride adorned for her husband" (Rev. 21:2). We are told the gates of the New Jerusalem are never shut, even though nothing defiled will ever enter therein. But what in the world (either this one or the next) is the New Jerusalem?

Chapter 4

The Kingdom of God:
Heaven, Paradise, New Jerusalem

One size does not fit all when it comes to defining the Kingdom of God, heaven, Paradise and the New Jerusalem. Each term represents a different facet of the whole revelation found in the gospel. When the different implications of each of these words are understood, the mist of confusion vanishes from the jumbled connections so often presented. This chapter will return to the foundational framework of these expressions so they can be understood and placed in proper context.

The Kingdom of God seems to be self-explanatory. A kingdom is a domain ruled by a king who is sovereign over his realm. To be in God's kingdom one must submit to the Lordship of the Father and His Son. Not to do so is to be outside this kingdom. But, unlike the kingdoms of this world, subjects are not forced into it, and they are free to leave because the Divine realm is spiritual. Those clinging to debased thoughts and attitudes will find themselves cast out because, "There shall by no means enter it anything that defiles, or causes an abomination or a lie (Rev 21:27). Those holding onto anything that would defile the kingdom must let go, before they can enter.

Although a child of the King, I have, at times, found myself standing outside the open gate. God is the Father of spirits (Heb. 12:9) and Truth. Access is through spirit and truth alone. Jesus taught it this way:

Now when He was asked by the Pharisees when the kingdom of God would come, He answered them and said, "The kingdom of God does not come with observation; nor will they say, 'See here!' or 'See there!' For indeed, the kingdom of God is within you" (Luke 17:20-1).

Some Bible commentators have said that the word *within* could be translated as *among*. However, the Greek word that is used in that passage is *entos,* and it only means within. There are other Greek words that could be translated either way, but they were not used in this passage. Also, the Pharisees were standing right there observing Jesus, so the word among, implying that Jesus was referring to Himself, would not make sense in the context of the passage. Jesus had just told them "the kingdom of God does not come with observation".

Jesus, being heir to the Father's kingdom, said, "My kingdom is not of this world. If My kingdom were of this world, My servants would fight, so that I should not be delivered to the Jews; but now My kingdom is not from here" (John 18:36). Jesus said that the physical man cannot even see the kingdom of God, let alone enter it (John 3:3-7). So the second coming of Christ cannot be to force compliance into His reign, onto those not born of the Spirit.

Yet, there is this prophecy in *Revelation*: "The kingdoms of this world have become *the kingdoms* of our Lord and of His Christ, and He shall reign forever and ever" (Rev. 11:15). Paul wrote to the Corinthians, "flesh and blood cannot inherit the kingdom of God" (I Cor. 15:50). So if the kingdoms of this world, which are flesh and blood dominions, are destined to become the kingdoms of our Lord and of His Christ, how is that realized? The previous verses answer, "As we have borne the image of the *man* of dust, we shall also bear the image of the heavenly *Man* "(I Cor. 15:49). This, of course, is referring to the likeness of His holy spiritual qualities or virtues first and foremost, as well as His glorified body. It is the Holy Spirit that conquers sin and the resulting death.

Paul expounds on bearing the image of Christ in other letters. "For whom he did foreknow, He also predestined *to be* conformed to the image of his Son... (Rom. 8:29). "But we all, with unveiled face, beholding as in a mirror the glory of the Lord, are being transformed into the same image from glory to glory, just as by the Spirit of the Lord" (II Cor. 3:18). This change is a spiritual resurrection currently in process, from glory to glory.

Paul was stressing to the believers that the Kingdom of God was not going to be the physical mortal reign that they had in mind. Its subjects would not be subdued by force (Luke 22:25). They would be conquered through love. In this way the kingdoms of this world become, through conversion, the kingdoms of our Lord and of His Christ from the inside to the outside. The Kingdom comes through progressive spiritual transformation from glory to glory as eternal life swallows death (II Cor. 5:4).

The growth of children frames a similar parallel. Children transforming into adults is not an easy process. The five-year-old has died by the time the twelve-year-old has emerged, and so on. Paul exhorted the disciples to continue in the faith: "We must through many tribulations enter the kingdom of God" (Acts 14:22).

First Corinthians 15 is about the necessity of death and resurrection, relating to this process of entering into the eternal Kingdom of God. Paul likens the method of transformation to a physical seed that must be planted in the ground and die before it can grow into the unique and glorious plant it was designed to be. The genetic code is in the seed, but the seed must die before the plant will blossom. The physical is in the ongoing process of dying, as it must return to the dust, while the spiritual is in the process of change and resurrection.

The expression *Kingdom of Heaven* is another revelation about the Kingdom of God. It would be absurd to suggest that God is not the sovereign authority of this kingdom. Therefore, it follows that the use of the term heaven is intended to reveal something about it other than who is king.

The word *heaven* is a translation of different words with similar connotations. In the Old Testament, the Hebrew word translated heaven is a word that literally means *heaved up things*. The root derivation of the English word heaven is heave. In the New Testament, the Greek word that is usually translated heaven literally means *sky* or *air*. So, in the literal sense it means that which is not bound to the earth. In the spiritual sense, it would represent lofty, moral or virtuous transcendent concepts like love, righteousness, or truth. This vocabulary does not represent a physical location. After all, flesh and blood cannot inherit the Kingdom of Heaven.

Jesus said, "No one has ascended to heaven, but he that came down from heaven, *that is,* the Son of Man who is in heaven" (John 3:13). If Jesus, while standing in the flesh on the earth, said He was in heaven, He must have been referencing a transcendent state that he was currently experiencing. Paul records, "He who descended is also the One who ascended far above all heavens, that He might fill all things" (Eph. 4:10). That is a curious way to describe ascension—to fill all things. It implies that when Christ ascended, He did not just rise bodily into the sky, He transcended it.

Jesus described the Kingdom of Heaven in metaphors and parables, identifying it with abstract spiritual realities instead of physical ones. Consider the parables that portray the Kingdom of Heaven as the seeds of the sower, the mustard seed, leaven, treasure in a field, or a net cast into the sea. These metaphors do not point to a physical location unless the kingdom is situated in a seed, bread, a field or the sea. The expression Kingdom of Heaven is meant to reveal that God's kingdom is one of high and lofty spiritual distinctions. People do not simply walk into the Kingdom; they grow into it. The death of the seed allows more space and freedom for the plant's continued growth.

The word *Paradise*, on the other hand, suggests a setting or environment. It is referenced only three times in the Bible, and the word itself means *park* or *garden grounds*. In context, each time the word Paradise is used in Scripture it implies a particular place, or location. The first instance is when Jesus was on the cross. Luke records that one of the thieves who was being crucified next to Christ turned to Him. "Then he said to Jesus, 'Lord, remember me when You come into Your kingdom.' And Jesus said to him, 'Assuredly, I say to you, today you will be with Me in Paradise'" (Luke 23:42-3).

Notice that Jesus changed the thief's frame of reference from Kingdom to Paradise. Jesus was already in His Kingdom, as it is a transcendent domain. The thief did not know exactly what he was asking, just as the mother of Zebedee's sons did not when she asked for them to sit on the right and left hands of Christ in His Kingdom. They were still thinking physical. Like the seed in Paul's analogy, the thief would have to grow into the kingdom. Yet, there would be plenty of nurturing help, as he would not be alone, but with Jesus in Paradise.

In the Kingdom of God, the greatest are servants, and they do not exercise authority as the world does (Luke 22:23-7). They exercise the greatest force in the universe—love. The power of love can summon great courage in the weakest and bring the mightiest to their knees. The greatest in God's Kingdom rule through its strength. So Paradise in that instance does not point to this metaphysical Kingdom. It implies that the man hanging next to Christ on the cross would be present with Him in a specific place that day.

The second instance is when Paul wrote about a man who may have had an out of body experience. "I know a man in Christ who fourteen years ago—whether in the body I do not know, or whether out of the body I do not know, God knows—such a one was caught up to the third heaven. And I know such a man—whether in the body or out of the body I do not know, God knows—how he was caught up into Paradise and heard inexpressible words, which it is not lawful for a man to utter" (II Cor. 12:2-4). We don't know what the man heard, but we can glean from this passage the man was in a particular place, where he could hear other beings talking.

The third instance is in *Revelation* and is quoted from the message to the church of Ephesus, "He who has an ear, let him hear what the Spirit says to the churches. To him who overcomes I will give to eat from the tree of life, which is in the midst of the Paradise of God" (Rev. 2:7). Each of these passages implies Paradise is a particular place or location, as opposed to the word heaven that literally connotes heaved up or air, something other than a place.

The description of the New Jerusalem implies, like heaven, that it is not a particular place. The word Jerusalem is a compound of the Hebrew words meaning foundation (or possession) and peace. So, *Jerusalem* literally means *foundation of peace*. In spite of the fact that the capital of Israel is called the City of Peace, it has seen very little peace throughout history. The city of Jerusalem has been besieged, captured and recaptured manifold times. However, the New Jerusalem is not that city.

John describes it in *Revelation*, and his description is quoted in its entirety here. It will present an overview, and the various symbolisms will be referenced throughout the rest of this chapter. "Then I, John, saw the holy city, New Jerusalem, coming down out of heaven from God, prepared as a bride adorned for her husband" (Rev. 21:2). The New Jerusalem is the bride of Christ, the church universal.

Later John writes a detailed allegorical description of Christ's bride using symbolisms the readers were familiar with from other parts of Scripture:

Then one of the seven angels who had the seven bowls filled with the seven last plagues came to me and talked with me saying, "Come, I will show you the bride, the Lamb's wife". And he carried me away in the Spirit to a great and high mountain, and showed me the great city, the holy Jerusalem, descending out of heaven from God, having the glory of God. Her light was like a most precious stone, like a jasper stone, clear as crystal. Also she had a great and high wall with twelve gates written on them, which are the names of the twelve tribes of the children of Israel: three gates on the east, three gates on the north, three gates on the south, and three gates on the west. Now the wall of the city had twelve foundations, and on them were the names of the twelve apostles of the Lamb. And he who talked with me had a gold reed to measure the city, its gates, and its wall. The city is laid out as a square; its length is as great as its breadth. And he measured the city with the reed: twelve thousand furlongs. Its length, breadth, and height are equal. Then he measured its wall: one hundred and forty-four cubits, according to the measure of a man, that is, of an angel. The construction of its wall was of jasper; and the city was pure gold, like clear glass. The foundations of the wall of the city were adorned with all kinds of precious stones: the first foundation was jasper, the second sapphire, the third chalcedony, the fourth emerald. The fifth sardonyx, the sixth sardius, the seventh chrysolite, the eighth beryl, the ninth topaz, the tenth chrysoprase, the eleventh jacinth, and the twelfth amethyst. The twelve gates were twelve pearls: each individual gate was of one pearl. And the street of the city was pure gold, like transparent glass (Rev. 21:9-21).

Again, the New Jerusalem is clearly identified as the bride of Christ. There is no guesswork. The prophet Isaiah wrote, "For *as* a young man marries a virgin, *so* shall your sons marry you; and as the bridegroom rejoices over the bride, so shall your God rejoice over you" (Isa. 62:5). The implication of the passage is that as God rejoiced over Jerusalem's sons, so Christ rejoices over His Church, the New Spirit filled Jerusalem.

Paul writes, "For I am jealous for you with godly jealousy. For I have betrothed you to one husband, that I may present you as a chaste virgin to Christ. But I fear, lest somehow, as the serpent deceived Eve by his craftiness, so your minds may be corrupted from the simplicity that is in Christ" (II Cor. 11:2-3). In that passage Paul, like John, described the church, the body of believers, as the bride of Christ.

Also note the passage refers to the *simplicity* of the gospel. This is a straightforward caution not to try to complicate His message. "For God is not *the author* of confusion but of peace, as in all the churches of the saints" (I Cor. 14:33). James writes, "For where envy and self-seeking exist, confusion and every evil thing are there. But the wisdom that is from above is first pure, then peaceable, gentle, willing to yield, full of mercy and good fruits, without partiality and without hypocrisy" (Jam. 3:16-17). So, the New Jerusalem should not be that complicated to understand within the context of previous revelation. Consider what other Scripture says about it.

The writer of *Hebrews* stated, "But you have come to Mount Zion and to the city of the living God, the heavenly Jerusalem, to an innumerable company of angels, to the general assembly and church of the firstborn who are registered in heaven, to God the Judge of all, to the spirits of just men made perfect, to Jesus the Mediator..." (Heb. 12:22-4). If we have already come to this city, then it must be a spiritual one, not a physical or literal place.

So again, the most logical interpretation is that the New Jerusalem is a symbolic reference to the church, the bride of Christ. The kingdom of God is the body of believers who have Christ within them ruling as king. This is also referred to as the *glory of God*. Since we have no glory in and of ourselves, that glory must be Christ in us. Paul clarifies, "To them God willed to make known what are the riches of the glory of this mystery among the Gentiles: which is Christ in you, the hope of glory" (Col. 1:27).

Consider the foundations of this city. Paul refers to Christians as God's building.

For we are God's fellow workers; you are God's field, you are God's building. According to the grace of God, which was given to me, as a wise master builder I have laid the foundation, and another builds on it. But let each one take heed how he builds on it. For no other foundation can anyone lay than that which is laid, which is Jesus Christ. Now if anyone builds on this foundation with gold, silver, precious stones, wood, hay, straw, each one's work will become clear; for the Day will declare it, because it will be revealed by fire; and the fire will test each one's work, of what sort it is (I Cor. 3:9-13).

Of course, gold, silver, and precious stones will withstand a fire better than wood, hay, and straw does. Most importantly, we—the church universal—are God's building and our foundation is Jesus Christ. Any work constructed on the foundation must be built with love, faith, and truth, things that will survive the refining fire of God.

Peter also referred to Christ and to the church as precious living stones. "Coming to Him as to a living stone, rejected indeed by men, but chosen by God and precious, you also, as living stones, are being built up a spiritual house, a holy priesthood, to offer up spiritual sacrifices acceptable to God through Jesus Christ" (I Pet. 2:4-5). Peter repeatedly emphasized that these stones are spiritual so that no one might misinterpret the metaphor as being a reference to anything physical. They are *living stones* being built into a *spiritual house*. The breastplate of judgment that the high priest of the temple was to bear upon his heart was set in twelve precious stones, each representing one of the tribes of Israel (Exodus 28). Hence, there is an ongoing metaphoric representation of precious stones throughout Scripture that the Jews would clearly understand.

Also, Jesus referred to believers as *light* in the Sermon on the Mount. "You are the light of the world. A city that is set on a hill cannot be hidden" (Matt. 5:14). John describes the New Jerusalem in *Revelation* as follows: "The city had no need of the sun or of the moon to shine in it, for the glory of God illuminated it. The Lamb is its light" (Rev. 21:22-3). Christ (the Lamb) in us is a light illuminating truth and understanding.

Revelation also tells us that the walls and gates of the New Jerusalem are measured. The number twelve comes up a couple times. The significance of that number is clarified in the vision. The twelve gates are the twelve tribes of Israel, and the twelve foundations are the twelve apostles. Some Bible commentators have suggested that since the city was measured, it must be taken as a description of a physical city. But the passage itself contradicts such a literal interpretation.

The significance of the fact that the dimensions of the city are 12 × 12, or 144, was interpreted and clarified in earlier passages from *Revelation*. It is the number of the servants of God who were sealed before the seventh seal was opened. "And I heard the number of those who were sealed. One hundred *and* forty-four thousand of all the tribes of the children of Israel were sealed" (Rev. 7:4). Later in *Revelation* that number is repeated.

> Then I looked, and behold, a Lamb standing on Mount Zion, and with Him one hundred and forty-four thousand, having His Father's name written on their foreheads. And I heard a voice from heaven, like the voice of many waters, and like the voice of loud thunder. And I heard the sound of harpists playing their harps. They sang as it were a new song before the throne, before the four living creatures, and the elders; and no one could learn that song except the hundred and forty-four thousand who were redeemed from the earth (Rev. 14:1-3).

Regarding the statement that the New Jerusalem was pure gold, Paul wrote to Timothy:

> But in a great house there are not only vessels of gold and silver, but also of wood and clay, some for honor and

some for dishonor. Therefore if anyone cleanses himself from the latter, he will be a vessel for honor, sanctified and useful for the Master, prepared for every good work (II Tim. 2:20-1).

There are also several Old Testament references to God's refining process as producing gold. Job declared, "But He knows the way that I take; when He has tested me, I shall come forth as gold" (Job 23:10). The prophet Zechariah wrote, "I will bring the one-third through the fire, will refine them as silver is refined, and test them as gold is tested. They will call on My name, and I will answer them. I will say, 'This is My people'; and each one will say, 'The Lord is my God'" (Zech. 13:9).

In the *Lamentations of Jeremiah*, gold is described as having lost its shine. "How the gold has become dim! *How* changed the fine gold! The stones of the sanctuary are scattered at the head of every street. The precious sons of Zion, valuable as fine gold, how they are regarded as clay pots, the work of the hands of the potter!" (Lam. 4:1-2). Gold never tarnishes like most other metals do, but it will stop shining if it is covered with grime, such as "the precious sons of Zion".

Understanding the common use of symbolism in Scriptures helps to clarify the visions and dreams recorded. If one is not familiar with the use of metaphoric language throughout Scripture, the interpretations of certain passages are open to anyone's guess. Perhaps, even worse, some people turn them into bizarre literal nonsense, as they try to make contemporary comparisons with writings directed to cultures thousands of years ago.

To explain the relationship between Christ and His church, Paul used the analogy of a marriage relationship.

For we are members of His body, of His flesh and of His bones. *"For this reason a man shall leave his father and mother and be joined to his wife, and the two shall become one flesh*". This is a great mystery, but I speak concerning Christ and the church" (Eph. 5:30-2).

Given that the New Jerusalem is the bride of Christ, consider the absurdity of a groom's obsession with literal silver and gold at His marriage. It is the bride who is important. It is the bride who is being described. Christ desires to become one mystically with the hearts of Adam's descendants; He desires to give them life. But how is this accomplished? Some, but not most of the historical church, claim it is through atonement by Christ's vicarious substitution for our punishment. But is that presupposed or imposed? And what is the inevitable theological consequence of such an assertion?

Chapter 5

Sacrifice and Substitution: The Great Schism

The doctrine of a substitutionary sacrifice is one of the most sacrosanct in Western theological thought. But few have a complete understanding of what it means or implies. Jesus died in our place, but we still die. Jesus took God's punishment for our sins, but our sins still have consequences. Consider the logical extension of the idea of a substitutionary paradigm. Is a vicarious victory really victory? Is vicarious righteousness really righteous? Is a vicarious life really life?

This chapter will cover the changing thoughts and theories about the concepts of *atonement* throughout history. It will unfold how we arrived at the contemporary idea of a vicarious substitutionary paradigm, and reveal the inherent problems with its logic and characterization of God.

History tells us, ancient people were prone to worship anything from golden calves to wooden images, and burning their innocent children in oblation to these gods was not uncommon. The early Hebrew nation was not immune from falling back into this practice (Jer. 7:31). The Old Testament use of animal sacrifices was the pre-ordained plan to put an end to human sacrifices, a pagan practice condemned throughout Scripture. It was the transformation period, which laid the groundwork to end all blood sacrifice. It pointed us to abstract spiritual realities. Christ ultimately made the final self- sacrifice in order to show us the true nature of God and to establish a higher spiritual form of worship through atonement, the Divine connection.

Scripture reveals that Jewish laws related to the structure and rituals of the temple were metaphoric, relating to God, eternal life, sin, and death (Heb. 9:9). Instead of buying favor through oblations, the new practices turned the Jew's focus toward sin, its destructive nature, and the ultimate cure for it.

The Biblical narrative from *Genesis* to *Revelation* is about this cure. That narrative advances through thousands of years and connects the varying empires through the Hebrew prophets. Prophetic fulfillment of the promised end to this system is evidenced by the fact that most of the world practiced blood offerings before Christ, and it is rarely practiced today. It is never practiced in Christianity.

The church has always been unified regarding the mystical workings of Christ's sacrifice. C.S. Lewis put it this way:

> The central Christian belief is that Christ's death has somehow put us right with God and given us a fresh start. Theories as to how it did this are another matter. A good many different theories have been held as to how it works; what all Christians are agreed on is that it does work" (*Mere Christianity*, 54).

I would propose the reason for varying views is that spiritual realities are transcendent. They can only be suggested at. Thus the struggle to communicate these truths calls for multiple analogies and various images. These symbols are like the alphabet. Children learn the letters of the alphabet and how they related to words before they are able to process words to sentences. Eventually they relate complete sentences to stories and ultimately to abstract ideas. The spiritual messages and lessons found in stories are the reason for the telling. But it all begins with an understanding of symbols.

To understand the atonement and its sacrificial connection, it must be examined in light of the entire Word of

God, the complete story. All early Hebrew symbolism must be utilized. Comprehensive focus must be maintained in order to avoid being unduly influenced by theological interpretations from isolated fragments of Scripture. As mentioned in Chapter 3, understanding the beauty of a rose cannot be accomplished by tearing it apart and searching for meaning in the individual components. The significance of the rose lies in the mystical meaning of it as a complete object. That cannot be perceived by focusing only on one petal or a leaf. I remember a school assignment my children once had requiring them to draw a picture of a dinosaur. About thirty students were given the same incomplete remnants of bones. The end result was thirty remarkably different images, each an individual interpretation of the same limited raw material.

Doctrinal thought has not been left untouched by a similar process of fragmentation. However, through two millennia of changing theological ideas, a common foundation has remained solid and unbroken. Man's sinful nature needs to be redeemed from a fallen state, disconnection from God. Christ was sent to mediate reconciliation and save us from sin.

To this day there is no universally accepted understanding of the atonement, as there is regarding most other major doctrines, such as the deity of Christ, the trinity, or the divine inspiration of the canon of Scripture. That is not to say there is no dissension among some regarding those (and other) doctrines, I would simply point out that such debates were addressed in the first few centuries following Christ and form a common foundation for all Christian religions. However, atonement paradigms have changed, and it would be wise to consider the implications of one's theology.

The earliest atonement theories, taught by Irenaeus, Athanasius, and others in the second century, held that the incarnation, God in Christ, was itself the atoning act. It was believed that restoring one human being to perfection restored the human nature of all, "For as in Adam all die, even so in Christ all shall be made alive" (I Cor. 15:22).

Other church fathers, such as Origen, believed that salvation from sin was obtained through the conquest of Satan in that Christ defeated the power of the devil through Calvary, "Having disarmed principalities and powers, He made a public spectacle of them, triumphing over them in it" (Col 2: 15). "You were bought at a price" (I Cor. 6:20), was understood to mean that a ransom was paid to the devil. "…the Son of Man did not come to be served, but to serve, and to give His life a ransom for many" (Matt. 20:28; Mark 10:45). It was believed that God was so good He always stood ready to forgive, requiring only repentance.

In the eleventh and twelfth centuries St. Anselm of Canterbury (1033 – 1109) and Peter Abelard (1079 – 1142), rejected Origen's position of a price being paid to the devil. Both Anselm and Abelard argued that since God was omnipotent, He could destroy the devil outright, and thus did not need such an extreme remedy as the incarnation. Anselm proposed that payment was made to God, not Satan, for the restitution of His offended "honor". Christ paid back the honor through obedience. He taught that since Christ's life was of incalculable worth, it was thus capable of making reparation for our sin.

Anselm's paradigm shift turned "God who has reconciled us to Himself through Jesus Christ…" (II Cor. 5:18) into God reconciling Himself to us. His position assumed the honor of God could somehow be offended, as if a toddler could tread on the esteem of a parent. Even if that were possible, how could the torture and death of anyone restore that honor? The question is glaring, as Anselm's argument is a *non sequitur* lacking logical connection.

Rejecting Anselm's position, Peter Abelard wrote in his *Exposition of the Epistle to the Romans*:

> If [the] sin of Adam was so great that it could be expiated only by the death of Christ, what expiation will avail for the act of murder committed against Christ, and for the many great crimes committed against him or his

followers? How did the death of his innocent Son so please God the Father that through it He should be reconciled to us—to us who by our sinful acts have done the very things for which our innocent Lord was put to death? (pp. 282-3, trans. Eugene R. Fairweather).

In that same exposition, Abelard expounded on those questions:

What expiation will avail for that act of murder committed against Christ? If His life was of infinite value, surely His execution was of infinite disvalue. Now it seems to us that we have been justified by the blood of Christ and reconciled to God in this way: through this unique act of grace manifested to us in that His Son has taken upon Himself our nature and persevered therein in teaching by word and example even unto death, He has more fully bound us to Himself by love; with the result that our hearts should be enkindled by such a gift of divine grace, and the true charity should not now shrink from enduring anything for Him (283).

Embracing Anselm, the Western church's debate over the meaning and purpose of Christ's sacrifice did not take another dramatic turn for an additional five hundred years when reformer John Calvin (1509 – 1564) first applied the word "substitution" to Scripture. Calvin, a lawyer, postulated that Christ satisfied God's "justice" by being punished in our place. Whereas Anselm focused on paying honor due as satisfaction, Calvin posited a penalty payment as substitution to satisfy the debt of honor owed.

Then around three hundred years later, R.C. Moberly (1845 – 1903) first used the words "vicarious penitence" to describe Christ's sacrifice. He reasoned that because Jesus was sinless, He could not substitute certain penalties such as guilt, remorse and repentance, which were an essential part of the law. Therefore, Moberly concluded, His penalty had to be "vicarious". In other words, Christ did not need to pay the exact literal punishment prescribed by law.

Today many Christians consider the crucifixion of Christ to be a substitutionary or vicarious sacrifice, that is, Christ paid the penalty for our sins by enduring God's wrathful punishment that we deserved. However, that was certainly not the interpretation for most of Western church history, nor is it for much of Eastern Orthodoxy today.

I always felt uneasy with that characterization of God and was relieved to discover that early church paradigms were more consistent with the nature of the Father revealed in Christ. The rest of this chapter will focus on the many passages used to support atonement by substitution and the inherent problems with that paradigm.

To begin, the sacrificial nature of Christ's crucifixion was understood as a provision, not a substitution, for the entire first millennium. God's sacrifice for His creation was like the sacrifice that parents make for their children. Parents continually sacrifice time, energy, and resources for their progeny in order to feed, instruct, discipline and comfort them. Good parents will protect their children from danger with their own lives. This is certainly not meant to diminish the horrendous torture of the crucifixion by analogy with parents giving of themselves for their children. It is only meant to clarify the meaning of sacrifice in relation to Christ's death. Sacrifice can simply describe provisional actions, unrelated to repayment of debt.

Small children do not owe their parents anything; rather, the parents are responsible for their children. They care for them simply because they love them and are accountable for them as a result of bringing them into this world. Every culture in the world acknowledges the responsibility of parental sacrifice for the interests of their offspring. As children are created in the image of their parents, so is mankind created by God and in the image of God.

As sons and daughters mature, honor is certainly due to their parents. But what parent would be satisfied with honor given by anyone other than his or her own child? What mother or father would be satisfied with the punishment of a third party as a replacement for the honor of their children? Could any parent's heart be satisfied with anything less than the mutual love and respect given from their very own child? Homage from the entire universe would not be a sufficient replacement. I was compelled to revisit all the Scriptures used to support Calvin and Moberly's paradigms along with the terminology and came away with some interesting insights.

Paul wrote, "For you were bought at a price; therefore glorify God in your body and in your spirit, which are God's" (I Cor. 6:20). This was the source of Anselm's and Abelard's divided opinions. To whom was this price paid? Asking that question may be something like asking what is the color of truth? It makes no sense if the price was not paid to someone else. A price often refers to the sacrifices one must make to accomplish something.

If one runs a race to receive a prize, the price paid is practice and self-discipline. It is not paid to anyone. If a woman wants to bring a baby into the world the price she pays is the pain of childbirth. To whom does she pay this? There is a price of time and effort paid to maintain friendships; it is not owed. The term *paid* is commonly used in expressions unrelated to debt. Consider its use in Francis Thompson's poem *Daisy*:

> Nothing begins, and nothing ends,
> That is not paid with moan;
> For we are born in other's pain
> And perish in our own.

Just as the word *paid* does not always apply to the settlement of a debt, the word *bear*, which is also often used in the substitutionary paradigm, does not always apply to removing someone else's burden. There are many Scriptural references to Jesus bearing our suffering and sin. But consider other similar usages of the word *bear* in the following analogies. Ezekiel was called to bear the iniquity of Israel (Chapter 4). The price he paid by bearing their sin was not a substitution for the righteousness the Israelites owed by their covenant to obey God. Ezekiel bore their sin to communicate, through a visual representation, a message from God. He sacrificed his comfort to give them something.

Another example of bearing sin would be one of a man who kills an innocent man over a disagreement. The dead man would be the one who bore the sin of the killer as Christ bore the sins of those who put him to death. When Pilate asked Jesus if He were a king, Jesus affirmed and said, "For this cause I was born, and for this cause I have come into the world that I should bear witness to the truth" (John 18:37). I might add it is significant that Jesus revealed the reason He came into the world. No guessing is involved. He never once mentioned being a placating sacrifice to appease an angry God. That would certainly be an essential fact to leave out.

The substitution paradigm contains two main logical fallacies. It asserts Christ's death substituted for our physical death and/or for our spiritual death. Christ cannot logically be a substitute for either. If you believe Jesus is the Son of God, His death cannot be a substitute for spiritual death because Jesus is the incarnation of eternal life. He cannot die spiritually without ceasing to be the essence of who He is.

Jesus' cry from the cross, *"My God, My God, why have You forsaken Me?"* (Matt. 27:45), has been interpreted by some as implying His death was a substitution for our spiritual death. A common theological interpretation of that Scripture is that God the Father abandoned His Son at the moment Christ uttered those words. He turned His back on His own Son, pouring out wrath that was meant for us onto Him. But, a more reasonable explanation would be that Jesus was quoting the first line of Psalm 22, as if He were directing people to look at that Psalm in light of the events of the crucifixion. Bear in mind that Jesus frequently quoted Scripture foretelling the significance of His life and death.

Jesus was, even at the time of His physical death, directing us to the prophetic fulfillment of events that were then taking place. The author of Psalm 22 is King David, and the verses that follow that cry *"My God, My God, why have You forsaken Me?"* prophetically describe in exact detail the events of the crucifixion. David writes, "They pierced my hands and my feet" (vs. 16). Christ's hands and feet were pierced. The exact words used to mock Jesus by onlookers are referenced, "He trusted in the Lord, let Him rescue Him; let Him deliver Him, since He delighted in Him!" (vs. 8). David predicts that His clothes would be divided among the Roman soldiers and that they would cast lots for His robe (vs. 18). Reflect on "I am poured out like water, and all my bones are out of joint" (vs. 14) as it relates to hanging on a cross. In the middle of the narrative, David continues with: "You have answered Me".

He concludes with the message that God has not forsaken the afflicted but will establish His kingdom through His affliction (Ps. 22:24-31). The crowning touch describes His deliverance through resurrection and the impact it would have on the world:

All those who go down to the dust shall bow before Him. Even he who cannot keep himself alive. A posterity shall serve Him. It will be recounted of the Lord to the *next* generation. They will come and declare His righteousness to a people who will be born, that He has done *this* (Ps. 22:29-31).

After pointing to this prophecy Jesus declared, "It is finished". The context is an account beginning with what looked like God's abandonment but finished with God's redemptive plan and purposes of the event. I would encourage everyone to study Psalm 22 in its entirety. It is an amazingly detailed description of Christ's crucifixion and resurrection written many generations before the event.

Additionally, Christ cannot be a substitute for physical death because we will all die. There can be no surrogate substitution for either spiritual or physical death. The penalty for sin, death, either has already been paid by us as we were born into spiritual death or will be paid by us when we experience physical death.

Some have argued that Christ's death substitutes for the second death mentioned in *Revelation*. "Then Death and Hades were cast into the lake of fire. This is the second death" (Rev. 20:14). The meaning of this passage was discussed in Chapter 2. Since Jesus was not one of those cast into the lake of fire, He could not have been a substitution for that death.

Assuming that punishment could somehow satisfy the law raises another question: How can Christ fulfill the law by substituting a punishment that is less than the law requires, unending torment as some affirm? If God can substitute something less or different from the established penalty required from us, then it stands to reason He could substitute no penalty at all. He could simply forgive and exercise mercy.

To say that God is shackled by a legal code that obligates Him to return evil for evil is to say that God is not sovereign. It reduces the significance of Christ's death to a mere business transaction. Furthermore, if the debt from the covenant has been cleared, there remains no need of forgiveness and mercy.

Unending suffering is often coupled with atonement by substitution. So if the penalty for sin is endless torment in hell, as some maintain, the substitution of Christ in our place is illogical since Jesus has ceased to suffer. Luke writes of Him, "whom God raised up, having loosed the pains of death, because it was not possible that He should be held by it" (Acts 2:24). Many people witnessed Christ's resurrected body, and the first martyr, Stephen, saw Christ "standing at the right hand of God" (Acts 7:56). So Christ is certainly not being tormented for sinners by taking their place in a fiery abyss. Nevertheless, even if He were still suffering, how could such a substitution or penance take away the sin, hence the pain, of the world? After all, sin creates suffering.

Those who profess the idea that God the Father poured out His wrath for our sin on His perfectly innocent Son often reference *Isaiah* 53. It is one of the most remarkable prophesies in Scripture. It contains the famous passage predicting the manner and means of the death of Christ on the cross, written over 700 years before the event.

Surely He has borne our grief and carried our sorrows; yet we esteemed Him stricken, smitten by God, and afflicted. But He *was* wounded for our transgressions, *He was* bruised for our iniquities; the chastisement for our peace *was* upon Him, and by His stripes we are healed. All we like sheep have gone astray; we have turned, every one, to his own way; and the Lord has <u>laid</u> on Him the iniquity of us all. (Isa. 53:4-6).

The word translated *laid* in that passage is the Hebrew word *pâga*, which is usually rendered *fall* or *meet*. *Young's Literal Translation (YLT)* of Isa. 53:6 reads, "And Jehovah hath <u>caused to meet</u> on him, the punishment of us all". The *Septuagint (LXX)* translates it, "The Lord <u>gave Him up</u> for our sins". Paul clarified the meaning of this Scripture. He wrote that Jesus was "delivered for our offenses and was <u>raised</u> again for our justification" (Rom. 4:25, KJV). Note that Christ's <u>resurrection</u> justified us—not His death.

The fact that God allowed (or caused) His Son's crucifixion because of our iniquity is a wholly different concept than God vicariously imputing our iniquity onto Him. The "punishment of us all" refers to the same punishment that every physical being must endure: *death*. Substitution here is illogical, since we all must still die.

Also, there is nothing in the Isaiah 53 passage to lead one to the interpretation that God caused the events of punishment to fall on His Son to satisfy His wrath or to fulfill an assumed law of justice. In fact, that idea is totally contrary to what Jesus taught. In the Parable of the Wicked Vinedressers, Jesus described a landowner who planted a vineyard and sent his servants to collect the fruit. But the vinedressers beat and killed the servants (Matt. 21:33-6).

> Then last of all he sent his son to them saying, "They will respect my son". But when the vinedressers saw the son, they said among themselves, "This is the heir. Come, let us kill him and seize his inheritance" (Matt. 21:37-8).

More insight on Christ's suffering is given in Heb. 5:8-9, "though He was a Son, yet He learned obedience by the things which He suffered. And having been perfected, He became the author of eternal salvation to all who obey Him". Since the Eternal Word of God was already perfect in Jesus, there remained only the completion of the human experience, which included suffering and death. Through this experience Christ became the sole mediator between man and God. He was perfectly connected to God and perfectly connected to man.

The character of Elihu in the book of *Job* portrays an intercessory parallel. Job, maintaining God is just and merciful, bemoans his inability to have his day in court with the Almighty and be exonerated. "For He is not a man, as I am, that I may answer Him, and that we should go to court together. Nor is there any mediator between us, who may lay his hand on us both" (Job 9:32-3). Later on in the narrative Elihu takes the stage and declares:

> Behold, I am according to thy wish in God's stead: I also am formed out of the clay. Behold, my terror shall not make thee afraid, neither shall my hand be heavy upon thee" (Job 33:6-7, KJV).

Note that Elihu is interceding on God's behalf as Jesus did. God wants to communicate something to Job. It is certain that God knows Job's situation and heart. He has been in an ongoing discussion with Satan about it and had already pronounced Job perfect and upright.

The prophet Isaiah writes, "Yet it pleased the Lord to bruise Him; He has put Him to grief" (Isa. 53:10). Some have concluded from this text that God took pleasure in the sacrificing of His Son to satisfy His wrath. But the most likely connotation of the word *pleased* in that passage is clarified later on in the same verse. "When you make His soul an offering for sin, He shall see His seed, He shall prolong His days, and the pleasure of the Lord shall prosper in His hand". Clearly it is the curative results of this entire event that the Lord desired. His pleasure results from the prospering seed not from the satisfaction that some arbitrary law of justice had been served.

Pleasure in placating sacrifices goes contrary to other passages throughout Scripture that say God does not enjoy sacrifices for sin. The Hebrew word *hapes* translated *pleased* in that verse is translated "wanted" or "desired" elsewhere in Scripture. It contains the same root word Isaiah uses a little later, "So shall My word be that goes forth from My mouth; it shall not return to Me void, but it shall accomplish what I please [want or desire]" (Isa. 55:11). Jesus, the "Word" of God incarnate, accomplished the results God desired. With that God was well pleased.

The fact that God does not take pleasure in human or animal sacrifices is made perfectly clear throughout Scripture. David wrote in *Psalms*:

> For You do not desire sacrifice, or else I would give it; You do not delight in burnt offering. The sacrifices of God are a broken spirit, a broken and a contrite heart—these, O God, You will not despise (Ps. 51:16-7).

God does not even take pleasure in the death of the wicked (Eze. 33:11). It is what the sacrifice accomplished that is pleasing, not the means. Paul wrote:

> And you, who once were alienated and enemies in your mind by wicked works, yet now He has reconciled in the

body of His flesh through death, to present you holy, and blameless, and above reproach in His sight—if indeed you continue in the faith, grounded and steadfast, and are not moved away from the hope of the gospel which you heard (Col. 1:21-3).

We were alienated from God, not God from us. After Adam and Eve disobeyed God by eating the forbidden fruit, they hid from Him (Gen. 1:8). The light of God was viewed as intruding. God in His love came looking for them. Redemption was promised; but they first needed to grasp the long-term consequences of avoiding Divine illumination. The ramifications are seen throughout the history of the world. Yet, God's compassionate pursuit of those who are lost and His offer of reconciliation do not cease.

Scripture teaches throughout that Jesus came to save us from our *sin*, not from the penalty for it. There is no salvation from penalty except through salvation from sin taught anywhere. Forgiveness for the repentant is taught everywhere, but forgiveness is not salvation. It will not cleanse us from our propensity to sin. It cannot purify our conscience, our inner thoughts (Heb. 9:14). God pardoned the Israelites for not trusting Him enough to fight the battles for the Promised Land. Nevertheless, they were unable to enter it (Num. 14:20-3). Forgiving my child for leaving lunch money behind does not guarantee he or she will not go hungry at the break.

When Joseph was struggling with the question of whether or not to leave Mary because she was pregnant, an angel of the Lord appeared to him and revealed the nature of the child she was carrying, "…And she will bring forth a Son, and you shall call His name JESUS, for He will save His people from their sins" (Matt. 1:21).

Contrary to some traditional hymns, sin is not a stain. In Scripture, the word usually translated as sin is *hamartia*, meaning to *err* or *miss the mark*. That mark is oneness, harmony or wholeness in God. The word translated *saved* is *sozo*, which may also be translated *to be made whole*. So, whereas sin is to miss the mark of wholeness, being saved is to achieve wholeness, that is, unity with God. The transcendent nature of discord with God produces harmful behavior.

Those actions cannot be divorced from their consequences. Consider the consequences of sin. If I kill my neighbor, the consequence is a dead person and all the ramifications that entails. The harm has already been done. It can only be reconciled and redeemed. The only way to take away sin is to stop it from occurring as past actions cannot be reversed. But repentance from such behavior can lead to restoration in the future.

Such experiences change the essence of who we are. I used to believe salvation was about a free ticket into a really happy place called heaven. I now understand it is about who I am becoming through Christ who is conforming me into His image through Divine connection (II Cor. 3:18). No place is truly *happy* unless it is free from sin and the suffering it causes.

Paul writes to the Romans, "the Kingdom of God is not eating and drinking, but righteousness and peace and joy in the Holy Spirit" (Rom 14:17). These are transcendent, spiritual qualities that cannot be purchased with money. Nor can they be obtained through our own labor or works. One cannot do chores, work at the office, or offer a sacrifice and then take home a box of righteousness, peace and joy. The kingdom is acquired through unity and harmony with God. As we hear and act in accordance with God and His Holy Spirit, we are infused with these attributes of God Himself (Titus 3:5).

Quoting a passage in Deuteronomy, Paul writes, "*Vengeance is Mine, I will repay, says the Lord.*" (Rom. 12:19). The word translated *vengeance* comes from the Greek word *ekdikesis,* which can be translated *vindication.* In other words, God will prove His Word right and true through the consequences of our own actions. There is a big difference between punishment for revenge and consequences.

Jesus clearly rejected violence as a path to righteousness. Since He is the Word of God incarnate, it would be illogical to claim that the Father achieves righteousness through violent recompense. From childhood I was taught and understood the old adage that two wrongs don't make a right. If you break my nose, breaking yours won't fix mine. Punishment does not justify (correct) injury. When properly administered for correction, it may lead to repentance and thus righteousness; but it cannot be a substitute for righteousness. Consider that we even call our prisons correctional institutions.

To assume God the Father needs to appease His wrath by taking it out on His innocent Son is contrary to His own definition of love. The character of God, reiterated throughout Scripture, is *agapé*, the self-sacrificing love that Christ taught and lived. One trait of *agapé* is it "seeks not its own way" (I Cor. 13:6). So, for God to revenge His offended honor by the bloody, brutal torture and death of Christ is completely contrary to that Divine nature. Again, it does nothing to restore honor.

The idea must be a projection, stemming from a legalistic propensity to desire gratification through retribution. If God is one who cares more about His adulation than a father cares for the growth and virtue of his children, we might well need such protection. But Jesus never alluded to any such disposition in the Father. Christ taught that Divine law was fulfilled by love, not punishment. A lawyer came to Christ and asked:

> "Teacher, which *is* the great commandment in the law?" Jesus said to him, *"You shall love the LORD your God will all your heart, with all your soul, and with all your mind. This is the first and great commandment. And the second is like it: You shall love your neighbor as yourself.* On these two commandments hang all the Law and the Prophets" (Matt. 22:36-40).

Paul reiterated that same principle in *Romans*, "Owe no one anything except to love one another, for he who loves another has fulfilled the law" (Rom. 13:8).

A rich young ruler enquired about what he must do to obtain eternal life. When he asserted he had kept the commandments from his youth up, Jesus did not deny this. Christ said he needed something more (Luke 18:22). This young ruler was unknowingly asking an illogical question. It was not something he must do to acquire eternal life, but rather something he must become. He would need to spend time with Jesus to understand that eternal life (heaven) is not the reward of virtue, it is virtue (righteousness, peace, and joy).

The law of God is spiritual and therefore cannot be fulfilled by adherence to the Mosaic traditions. Jesus broke the Mosaic Law, yet fulfilled the spiritual law by healing on the Sabbath. That is why Paul declared he was faultless regarding the Law of Moses. Zacharias and Elizabeth "were both righteous before God, walking in all the commandments and ordinances of the Lord blameless" (Luke 1:6).

So the gospel message is not that Christ fulfilled the Mosaic Law and substituted our punishment. The message is the Law is transcendent and fulfilled by the love of God shed abroad in our hearts through Divine union with the Holy Spirit. In *Creation in Christ* George MacDonald inserts a long quote from an unidentified writer in this passage:

> I have been led to what I am about to say, by a certain utterance of one in the front rank of those who assert that we can know nothing of the "Infinite and Eternal energy from which all things proceed," and the utterance is this:
>> The visiting of Adam's descendants through hundreds of generations dreadful penalties for a small transgression which they did not commit; the damning of all men who do not avail themselves of an alleged mode of obtaining forgiveness, which most men have never heard of; and the effecting a reconciliation by sacrificing a son who was perfectly innocent, to satisfy the assumed necessity for a propitiatory victim; are modes of action which,

> ascribed to a human ruler, would call for expressions
> of abhorrence; and the ascription to them to the
> Ultimate Cause of things even now felt to be full of
> difficulties, must become impossible.
> I do not quote the passage with the design of opposing
> either clause of its statement, for I entirely agree with it.
> Almost it feels an absurdity to say so. Neither do I
> propose addressing a word to the writer of it, or to any
> who hold with him. The passage bears out what I have
> often said—that I never yet heard a word from one of that
> way of thinking, which even touched anything I hold. One
> of my earliest recollections is of beginning to be at strife
> with the false system here assailed. Such paganism I scorn
> as heartily in the name of Christ, as I scorn it in the name
> of righteousness (94).

Scripture does not support the idea that God created man
with an inherited sinful nature after Adam and then required
an innocent propitiatory victim to punish for that fallen nature.
It took over an entire millennium before that paradigm could
be contrived out of the Bible. In fact, the killing of an innocent
person is condemned throughout Scripture.

Punishment by substitution is specifically forbidden by
the Old Testament legal code. In *Deuteronomy* we read,
"Fathers shall not be put to death for *their* children, nor shall
children be put to death for *their* fathers; a person shall be put
to death for his own sin" (Deut. 24:16). For God to require the
stand-in death of someone innocent for the sins of others
would violate His own law. You cannot fulfill a law by
transgressing it.

The prophet Micah also corrects the mistaken belief that
sacrifice is somehow an appeasement to God.

> With what shall I come before the LORD, and bow myself
> before the High God? Shall I come before Him with burnt
> offerings, with calves a year old? Will the Lord be
> pleased with thousands of rams, ten thousand rivers of

oil? Shall I give my firstborn for my transgression, the fruit of my body for the sin of my soul? He has shown you, O man, what is good; and what does the LORD require of you but to do justly, to love mercy, and to walk humbly with your God" (Mic. 6:6-8).

When the Israelites began to believe God was somehow placated by these sacrifices, like the pagans believed their gods were, He sent numerous prophets to correct them. Isaiah wrote:

"To what purpose *is* the multitude of your sacrifices to Me?" says the LORD. "I have had enough of burnt offerings of rams and the fat of fed cattle. I do not delight in the blood of bulls, or of lambs or goats. When you come to appear before Me, who has required this from your hand to trample My courts?" (Isa. 1:11-2).

Also, Jeremiah prophesied:

For I did not speak to your fathers, or command them in the day that I brought them out of the land of Egypt, concerning burnt offerings or sacrifices. But this is what I commanded them, saying: Obey My voice and I will be your God, and you shall be My people. And walk in all the ways that I have commanded you, that it may be well with you'" (Jer. 7:22-3).

The *Book of Proverbs* declares, "The sacrifice of the wicked *is* an abomination to the LORD, but the prayer of the upright is His delight" (Prov. 15:8). In other words, sacrifice is not a substitution for righteousness. Jesus taught, "Therefore if you bring your gift to the altar, and there remember that your brother has something against you, leave your gift there before the altar, and go your way. First be reconciled to your brother, and then come and offer your gift" (Matt. 5:23-4).

The prophet Hosea summed up God's attitude toward sacrificial offerings: "For I desire mercy and not sacrifice, and the knowledge of God more than burnt offerings" (Hos. 6:6). The importance of that statement is driven home when Jesus quoted it rebuking the Pharisees: "Go and learn what this means, '*I desire mercy and not sacrifice*,' for I did not come to call the righteous, but sinners, to repentance" (Matt. 9:13).

If such oblations do not placate God, why were they instituted? To understand that it may be necessary to remove some preconceived filters and take a more diligent look. How were they related to the promised Messiah? What did Jesus accomplish through His life, death, and resurrection? I scoured the entire Bible in search of the words substitution and vicarious, but to no avail. My search continued for the equivalent idea through context. I discover that I had projected many presupposed ideas regarding substitution onto fragments of Scripture. I realized my need to reread the entire Bible, paying close attention to passages I assumed reflected a substitution paradigm.

Once again, I was surprised. The words *atoning*, *reconciliation*, and *redemption* are used to describe what was achieved. But there were no passages, when read in context, which even alluded to a substitution paradigm. Adding interpretation upon interpretation is a dangerous endeavor. It can only lead further away from the Divine mystery of the original Word. This is like the children's game of telephone, where a message is whispered to one person who then whispers it to the next person and the repetition goes from person to person around the room. When the last person to receive the message repeats what he or she heard, it is usually a completely different message from the original. I found I had incorporated contemporary associations, unintended by the authors, into Scripture. No wonder so many passages seemed confusing.

I began looking to the Bible itself for interpretation. Why was such an elaborate system of worship established? Why not just slaughter the sacrifices in the simplistic fashion of other pagan religions? Because the Hebrew practices were metaphors pointing to the spiritual nature of Christ's sacrifice. They were the letters, words and stories relaying spiritual concepts.

Blood is a foundational metaphor representing life throughout the Bible, as flesh is representative of sin and death. This analogy was established very early on (Lev. 17:11, Deut. 12:23). My association of blood with death, rather than life, kept me mystified in my attempts at integrating and understanding Scripture. This realization was the key I needed to unlock and make sense of the complete historical narrative. The communion wine of the New Testament becomes the life of Christ poured out that we must drink of and assimilate. Blood represents life, not death. God is not blood (death) thirsty; He is blood (life) thirsty. But how does blood as life pertain to the Old Testament system? The writer of Hebrews tells us that the sacrificial blood offered signified the Holy Spirit, (Heb. 9:7).

Sacrifice was a public forum for acknowledging sin, repentance, reconciliation and covenant—as opposed to the pagan practice of attempting to buy favor, or appease. Jesus told the leper he healed to go and make his offering as Moses had commanded, for a testimony (Luke 5:14). The Psalmist wrote, "Gather My saints together to me, those who have made a covenant with me by sacrifice" (Ps. 50:5). Paul wrote, "...for by the law is the knowledge of sin" (Rom. 3:20). The writer of *Hebrews* affirms, "But in those sacrifices there is a reminder of sins every year. For it is not possible that the blood of bulls and goats could take away sins" (Heb10: 3-4).

Like Ezekiel's sacrifice, these oblations served as prophecies and symbols of spiritual realities. In particular, they pointed to the Messianic promise of Christ. Although there were many different types of allegorical Old Testament oblations, the two main prototypes of Christ's offering were the Passover and the Atoning sacrifices.

The Passover was celebrated to "Remember this day in which you went out of Egypt, out of the house of bondage; for by strength of hand the Lord brought you out of this place" (Exodus 13:3). God's strength is the emphasis of this occasion as established in this passage and elsewhere.

The lamb offered was to be a male without blemish. Sins were not transferred to this lamb, and it was to be slain by the assembly. Christ, being sinless, was condemned to die by the assembly as they repeatedly shouted crucify him. The blood, symbolizing life (Lev. 17:11), was marked on the doorposts of those homes in Egypt that the angel of death was to pass over. Atonement was not mentioned here. Again, the emphasis is on the strength of God's power, the power of resurrection life in Christ. Paul tells us, "Christ our Passover was sacrificed for us" (I Cor. 5:7).

Christ offered the spiritual sacrifice of righteousness, "through the eternal spirit" (Heb. 9:14), and therefore death could not hold Him. Eternal life conquered death. Of course He had to pass through the *veil* of his flesh to accomplish this (Heb. 10:20). It was necessary to live and die in order to demonstrate power over death by way of eternal resurrection life. In II Peter 1:4, we are told that through Christ "you may be partakers of the divine nature". God's Divine nature has the power to save us from the slavery of Egypt (sin) and the power of death sin holds.

The second prototype was the atoning sacrifice. It was a yearly offering for the nation's sins of *ignorance*. Two goats were presented. One of the goats served as a sin offering, and again, no sins were transferred to this goat. A sin-laden sacrifice would not have been acceptable. The high priest was to kill this goat himself and sprinkle the blood, representing life (Lev. 17:11), within the veil of the tabernacle, upon the mercy seat. So, Christ entered the Holy of Holies through the veil of his flesh and offered his blood (life) upon the mercy seat.

This was a living sacrifice. The mercy seat is sprinkled with life inside the Holy of Holies, the inner sanctuary of the temple, beyond the veil. *Hebrews* tells us we can boldly enter into the "holiest" (the presence of God), "by the blood of

Jesus, by a new and living way which He consecrated for us, through the veil, that is, His flesh" (Heb. 10:19-20). His flesh is the veil, and His blood (life) is the atoning offering acceptable to God. We enter the Father's presence through the life of Christ. His death, of course, was the sacrifice necessary to demonstrate the power of His Divine Life over death. Jesus said "I lay down My life that I may take it again" (John 10:17).

The Day of Atonement did not end here. After the high priest finished his reconciling, the second goat was presented. The priest placed his hands on the head of the live goat and confessed the sins of the people, putting them on the head of the goat. This goat was sent away into the wilderness bearing the iniquities into a land not inhabited. "For as the heavens are high above the earth, great is His mercy toward those who fear Him. As far as the east is from the west, so far has He removed our transgressions from us" (Ps. 103:11-2). This represents what some call the process of sanctification. So, first atonement is made, then God can "work in you both to will and to do for His good pleasure" (Phil. 2:13), purifying your conscience (inner thoughts) from sin.

There were many other offerings outside of the Christ prototypes with various additional metaphoric messages. The key to comprehending the analogies lies in understanding that the only sacrifices acceptable to God are living ones. Flesh was never taken into the Holy of Holies for offering. Only the blood representing life was acceptable. The death served as a reminder of sin and its effects. "For if you live according to the flesh, you shall die" (Rom. 8:13).

The writer of *Hebrews* explains, "According to the law almost all things are purified with blood, and without shedding of blood there is no remission" (Heb. 9:22). This verse is often cited, out of context, as proof that Christ's crucifixion was necessary as a punitive substitution, rather than part of a provisional means for providing Divine Life to conquer sin and death.

Because of the assorted analogies the writer of *Hebrews* presents, it is paramount that these passages are read within their proper context. The topic of this passage begins in verse 15. The analogy establishes Christ as the testator of a will or testament. That is the New Testament, which is to be put in force after the death of the testator. As in all wills, the inheritance is not distributed until after the death of the one who established it. The inheritance of the Holy Spirit, which enables us to become partakers of the Divine nature, cannot be allocated until after the death of the Son. Only the Son is the rightful heir, able to distribute the inheritance.

So without the shedding of blood (Christ's eternal life sprinkled on the mercy seat inside the Holy of Holies) there is no remission (sending away) of sins. A trust fund or will is the narrative context and symbolism. The Son must first pass through the veil of His flesh offering His blood (life) to God. After His death, the "eternal" inheritance is distributed to us. That inheritance is the Holy Spirit, which was the estate of Christ, passed on to His beneficiaries at His death. Through this endowment of the Holy Spirit (God working in us) our sins are remitted (sent away) like the goat sent into the wilderness. We need the power of God's Holy Spirit in our lives to take away sin. It is a journey in process as represented by the scapegoat. There is no mention of, nor any allusion to a vicarious substitution in the passage anywhere. *Hebrews* clearly explains the metaphoric connection of shedding Christ's blood (life) and remission (*aphesis*, sending away) of sin.

The writer of *Hebrews* quotes the prophet Jeremiah, *"This is the covenant that I will make with them after those days, says the* LORD; *I will put My laws into their hearts, and in their minds I will write them"* (Heb. 10:16). The difference in the two covenants lies in the gift of Divine assistance through the Holy Spirit. The Divine life of Christ is sprinkled on the mercy seat over the New Jerusalem. In the Old Testament, Jerusalem is referred to as a tabernacle (Isa. 33:20). This was the physical parallel to the spiritual New Jerusalem, the bride of Christ, discussed in Chapter 4.

The book of *Hebrews* makes several other analogies. None mention that Jesus' suffering and death was to appease the Father's wrath. That silence speaks volumes. It would be too important of a concept to simply be left out. Not once did Jesus mention it. The life and death of Christ is described throughout Scripture as sacrificial, atoning, reconciling, redemptive, and restorative, but it is never described as a substitution for divine retribution.

Paul sheds some light on the nature of atonement in his letter to the church of the *Colossians*:

> And you, who once were alienated and enemies in your mind by wicked works, yet now He has reconciled in the body of His flesh through death, to present you holy, and blameless, and above reproach in His sight— (Col. 1:21-2).

The lost, disoriented, hostile and ailing world is reconciled— not God. God is not reconciled to the world.

Jesus taught the same in the parables he told of the prodigal son, the lost sheep, the lost coin, and the vineyard landlords who wanted to keep the owner's inheritance. He never taught the Father's anger would be appeased by His death or that a legal transaction, initiated by God, would be paid by God. What would be the point in telling your children they cannot have dessert until they eat their vegetables, but you will eat their vegetables for them? The price necessary to reconcile us was the incarnation and resurrection hence the physical death. The means of Christ's death, which was crucifixion, served the purpose Jesus asserted, "And I, if I am lifted from the earth will draw all to Myself" (John 12:32).

Before His death, Jesus prayed, "O My Father, if it is possible, let this cup pass from me; nevertheless, not as I will, but as you will" (Matt. 26:36). This passage is often quoted as proof that God required a propitiatory sacrifice to satisfy His requirement of *justice*. There was no other way. Why else would the Father not accommodate the prayer of his faithful Son? Later in the same chapter Jesus Himself clarified the necessity. When He was being arrested in Gethsemane, Jesus told His followers to put away the sword, and said:

> Do you think that I cannot now pray to My Father, and He will provide me with more than twelve legions of angels? How then could the Scriptures be fulfilled, that it must happen thus? (Matt. 26:53-4).

The passage concludes, "But all this was done that the Scriptures of the prophets might be fulfilled" (Matt. 26:56). There was no other way to fulfill the prophecies that were to identify Jesus as the promised Christ.

The Old Testament is replete with detailed prophecies concerning the life and manner of death of the Messiah. It was how we were to recognize that Jesus was the Messiah, the Christ we were to hear and obey, the Word of God incarnate. It was to separate Him from all the false self-proclaimed messiahs. No one but God could have brought to pass the fulfillment of so many varied and specific prophesies in one man. Indeed, there was no other way. All that was accomplished up to that point would have been wasted.

Up to that point God spoke through the prophets who foretold the coming promise of the Holy Spirit and redemption. While waiting, the ordinance of an "eye for eye, tooth for tooth" (Lev. 24:20) was meant to restrain the community from punishing an offender in a manner greater than the offense, thus ending the cycle of escalating retaliation. Excessive punitive damage compensation was forbidden. Not yet having the spiritual law of love and the Holy Spirit in their hearts they needed a natural law. This law was inferior to the spiritual law. It was a transitional law. Paul said, concerning the righteousness in the Old Testament law, he was blameless (Phil. 3:6). Yet, it was not enough to attain resurrection from the dead (Phil. 3:11).

One of the first steps towards God's *tsedaka* (translated *justice*, but having Divine implications, see Chapter 1) was not to escalate retaliation, Mafia style. In due time, Jesus taught a higher principle than Old Testament law. In the Sermon on the Mount He said:

> You have heard that it was said, "An eye for an eye and a tooth for a tooth". But I tell you not to resist an evil person. But whoever slaps you on your right cheek, turn the other to him also. If anyone wants to sue you and take away your tunic, let him have your cloak also. And whoever compels you to go one mile, go with him two. Give to him who asks you, and from him who wants to borrow from you do not turn away (Matt. 5:38-42).

From our limited perspective, these instructions sound difficult and lacking in justice. They do not represent our nature. However, Jesus clarified why we should follow them. "Therefore you shall be perfect, just as your Father in heaven is perfect" (Matt. 5:48).

Why are we to obey the directives of the Son? So we can be like our Father when we grow up. The Sermon on the Mount is a portrait of God. Why did Jesus endure such hateful treatment? He bore it because He was the express image of God (Heb. 1:3). It appears God is willing to endure deplorable disrespect and appalling abuse to buy our hearts back to Him and save us from the sin that is destroying us.

In conclusion, a paradigm of atonement through substitution creates schisms in the Bible's Divine message of God's love, forgiveness and redemption. So how do we put all the pieces together?

Chapter 6

Atonement:
Putting the Pieces Together

For a word that has been used as a synonym for unity with God, some current and historical explanations of *atonement* appear quite scrambled. Reconciliation has been muddled with salvation, forgiveness, redemption, and legalism. Trying to understand the meaning of multiple metaphors can be like trying to see the picture of a jigsaw puzzle with all the pieces overlapping. This chapter will separate and differentiate the terms, put the pieces in place, and complete the puzzle.

Atonement is a synonym for reconciliation, which literally means to win over to a friendly attitude. As used in a theological context, it refers to souls being won over (atoned) to God, not God being atoned to man (See Chap. 5). "God was in Christ reconciling the world to Himself, not imputing their trespasses to them, and has committed to us the word of reconciliation" (II Cor. 5:19).

Jesus clearly stated the reason He came, and He never mentioned purchasing the favor of the Father for us by taking our punishment. Standing before Pilot He said, "For this cause I was born, and for this cause I have come into the world, that I should bear witness to the truth" (John 18:37). Earlier in the gospel of *John* Jesus testified, "I am the light of the world. He who follows me shall not walk in darkness, but have the light of life" (John 8:12). Paul expressed Christ's purpose this way, "to give the light of the knowledge of the glory of God in the face of Jesus Christ" (II Cor. 4:6). Jesus was the sin offering, which was sacrificed for sins of *ignorance*. Through His sacrifice we have been given the light of the knowledge of God.

The Father freely forgives the repentant as Jesus taught in the Parable of the Prodigal Son. But forgiveness does not guarantee atonement or salvation; it is only a part of the process. Forgiveness does not save from sin; repentance and atonement do. Sin has ramifications. I grew up with a brother who was a drug addict. I loved him and forgave all abuses inflicted on me and my family. I claimed no retribution. But that did not save him from the results that led to his death. The fact that God forgives does not mean the rest of the world will, or that the laws of cause and effect will be removed, or that the eternal fires will cease to burn our hearts.

In other words, forgiveness is not salvation from sin, and is no guarantee to the heavenly kingdom of righteousness, peace and joy. So what then is the importance of forgiveness? First, there can be no atonement without it. But reconciliation requires at least two persons, while forgiveness only needs one. Forgiveness is neither atonement nor salvation. It is simply one step in the process. There can be no salvation without atonement, and no atonement without forgiveness. Scripture teaches our hearts, souls, and spirits would fail before God without His pardon (Isa. 57:16-8). Who would feel safe enough to approach God for the help and healing we need without knowing He is merciful? Most importantly, it is simply the natural outcome of love.

Forgiveness cannot be purchased with punishment. Many who have paid a life for a life have gone unforgiven by the victim's family. In the case of lesser crimes, such as theft, paying what is owed negates the necessity of a pardon. Forgiveness cannot be bought. It must be given freely, and love never fails to forgive the repentant. It never returns evil for evil.

This type of legalistic thinking, that the Father is unable to pardon without requiring offsetting punishment, is flawed by its own legal approach. The covenant between God and Israel, or God and His Church, are marriage covenants. Israel's part in the covenant was to keep the commands. God's part in the covenant was to be Israel's God if they obeyed His voice (Jer. 7:22-3). Disobedience simply permitted nullifying the promise if God chose. It did not "require" a divorce, or any other form of punishment to allow for forgiveness or reconciliation.

Furthermore, God is sovereign. As the Creator of the law, He is not Himself bound by the law. God is free to forgive and exercise mercy as He wills. Jesus said, "The Son of man is Lord even of the Sabbath" (Matt. 12:8). To be Lord of the Sabbath is to possess authority or rule over the Sabbath law and therefore all Mosaic law. The law was for our benefit. Imagine a parent setting a curfew for their child. Are the parents bound by that curfew also? If the child having broken the restriction is contrite, are the parents bound to punish anyway? No, the parents are not under the curfew, and they are free to pardon at will. Political leaders are free to do the same.

When Christ *purchased* us with a great price, He purchased *us*, our hearts, not forgiveness. How is this language to be understood in connection with other Scripture? In Biblical words, Jesus *redeemed* or *ransomed* us. These expressions are drawn from Old Testament analogies.

One parallel of particular significance is found in *Job*. Elihu, a Christ figure whose name means *God Himself*, declares, "Behold I am according to thy wish in God's stead: I also am formed out of the clay. Behold my terror shall not make you afraid…" (Job 33:6-7, KJV). Some interpretations make this appear as if Elihu is acting in Job's stead. However, such an interpretation is questionable in the context of the story. Job wants an answer to his suffering from God but is afraid because he mistakenly believes God is unfairly punishing him. Elihu states since he is also a man his presence will not frighten Job. Note that this would be an unnecessary comment if Elihu were going to relay Job's message, not the other way around. So, like Elihu, Christ came to bring God's heart and intent to us.

Elihu expounds on the mysterious ways of God, and the helpless state of mankind. He chides Job for striving against God's sovereignty. He states that when a man is in error as Job was in his ignorance of the situation, a messenger, or interpreter, can ransom or make atonement (Job 33:23-4), The word *ransom*, which is also rendered *atonement* in some translations, is derived from the Hebrew word *kopher* which is to cover. A cover serves as protection.

Here is the context: Elihu declares, if a man hearing the messenger turns to God, (again, the message is from God to man), that man will be restored to his righteousness. Remember Job in the beginning of the story had been declared blameless and upright. It is ultimately repentance that restores. Turning to God begins the process of atonement, *kopher,* that restores Job to his previous blameless state. Turning back to God protects a man from sin and thus its consequences. The messenger, as mediator of the process, is the redeemer who buys back the heart of the lost.

Scripture states Jesus came to save us from our sins, not from the consequences of our sins. To be saved from the hell of sin's effects, one has to cease from engaging in it. So the mediator redeems (buys us back) with the message of the Father's welcoming heart. The mercy of God leads to repentance, and repentance leads to reconciliation. This atonement/ransom/cover begins the process of saving us from sin.

I am often asked, "If Christ's death was not a substitution for our punishment, why was it necessary?" It was through death that Jesus, the second Adam, demonstrated the power of eternal life over sin and death. Jesus said, "I lay down My life that I may take it again" (John 10:17). He drew the world's attention to the sacrificial nature of God through the events of His crucifixion, as He said he would. The world's rejection of God was exposed, and His Word was vindicated through the resurrection. Finally, He fulfilled the messianic prophesies found in the metaphors of the laws and prophets regarding this sacrificial event.

His death was one part of the many things he did to reconcile us back to God. Scripture teaches: He brought the true face of the Father to us by bearing witness in words and deeds, even unto death, the accurate representation of the transcendent God in human flesh. We could not see that without Him. He showed us the way of true righteousness. We did not know the spiritual path. He fulfilled all Old Testament prophecies that identified Him as Messiah. He ascended to "fill all things" bestowing the promised divine power of His Holy Spirit life into the hearts of those who receive Him. To receive or believe in Jesus is to receive His word and testimony as truth.

The writer of *Hebrews* tells us that Jesus was the brightness of God's glory and the express image of His person (Heb. 1:3), an accurate portrayal of the Father. Trying to interpret Scripture when starting with an inaccurate foundational presupposition, such as a God whose anger is appeased by human or animal sacrifices, will surely lead to error. Our interpretation of Paul's epistles, the Old Testament, and other symbolic passages must remain consistent with the revelation given through the Divine Savior.

What did He teach about forgiveness? A penal substitutionary paradigm was never taught by Christ. That teaching renders His message backwards and inconsistent with the gospel. It portrays the crucifixion as an illustration of God's inability to forgive without exacting retribution. Jesus never displayed such character, or spoke of it as existing in the Father. In fact, Christ spoke against the legalism of such retaliation because it was our time to advance morally from the physical to the spiritual. Love has no restrictions on forgiveness.

Quoting Dr. Kalomiros again from *The River of Fire*, "To say that God turns away from the wicked is like saying the sun hides itself from the blind". Dr. Kalomiros explains the cause of this blindness: "Sin is the dark cloud which does not permit God's light to reach our eyes." The purpose of Christ coming was to save us from this spiritual pall. Christ fulfilled God's plan for our reconciliation by:

1. His life (His teaching and example) – "Christ also suffered for us, leaving us an example, that you should follow His steps" (I Pet. 2:21).
2. His death (by crucifixion) – "And I, if I am lifted up from the earth, will draw all to Myself" (John 12:32).
3. His resurrection (proof of who He was) "...declared to *be* the Son of God with power according to the Spirit of holiness, by the resurrection from the dead" (Rom. 1:4).
4. His ascension (filling all things) – "He who descended is also the One who ascended far above all heavens, that He might fill all things" (Eph. 4:10).
5. His indwelling of us (sanctification) – "To them God willed to make known what are the riches of the glory of this mystery among the Gentiles: which is Christ in you, the hope of glory" (Col. 1:27).
6. That we may know the Father (reconciliation) - "And this is eternal life, that they may know You, the only true God, and Jesus Christ whom You have sent" (John 17:3).

Atonement was not accomplished by a single act; it is a multifaceted process, each aspect inseparable from the rest. Nowhere does Scripture teach that one must believe in a vicarious righteousness to obtain salvation. It is taught everywhere to believe in Jesus, the Word of God. If righteousness were vicarious, or obtained through belief in a particular doctrinal creed, it would be outside of Christ and not in Him. Generations of Christians would be lost through believing various and changing doctrinal paradigms.

In *Creation in Christ* George MacDonald explains what is meant by the expression, "Christ is our righteousness".

Christ is our righteousness, not that we should escape punishment, still less escape being righteous, but as the live potent creator of righteousness in us, so that we, with our wills receiving His spirit, shall... know in ourselves, as He knows, what a lovely thing is righteousness, what a mean ugly, unnatural thing is unrighteousness. He is our righteousness, and that righteousness is not fiction, not pretense, no imputation (11).

We are not good people by nature, nor are we good people by proxy. Unless the Creator of Righteousness is alive in us, we have no hope of salvation. Christ's Word/Spirit is the righteousness we receive—bringing into being our righteousness out of His.

There are many Scriptures that assert we are justified by faith. The question is, faith in what? I have been told, faith in the finished work of Christ. Which finished work I ask. His bearing witness to the truth? "I have glorified thee on the earth: I have finished the work which thou gave me to do", was spoken by Jesus *before* his crucifixion (John 17:4). His death did not justify us. He was raised for our justification, delivered for our offenses. (Rom. 4:25). His reconciling of all things to himself? That would be a faith in the promised future. I have never read a word of Scripture stating I needed to have faith in what Jesus finished. Everywhere I read I must believe in Him, trust what He said. "Who is he that overcomes the world, but he that believes that Jesus is the Son of God," (I John 3:5), not he who believes in the finished work of Christ.

What does *justification by faith* mean in context with other Scriptures that maintain we must be obedient, persevere, and overcome to inherit the Kingdom of God? The definition of *justify* can be to either make or to proclaim right. To simply proclaim us righteous, when we in actuality are not, would be a lie. That would make salvation from sin an illusion and God a liar. He must first make us right before proclaiming us so, if the statement is to be grounded in reality.

The word translated *justify* is *dikaioo*. It may logically be understood as *declaring right* when used in a statement such as, "you... justify yourselves before men, but God knows your hearts" (Luke 16:15). Clearly there is no truth intended in the usage here, and the justification is condemned as false and misleading. But God cannot abide such contradiction, for He is truth. So *dikaioo* must be translated as *making right* in statements such as, it is God who justifies the ungodly or we are justified by faith. We are corrected by faith in what He told us to do. Faith is active and ongoing as is the virtue it produces. So we are actively being justified (made right, corrected, aligned with God and His purposes) through faith in Christ, the Word of God.

Atonement is often confused with salvation but Paul made a distinction in the terminology: "For if when we were enemies we were reconciled to God through the death of His Son, much more, having been reconciled, we shall be saved by His life" (Rom. 5:10). We were reconciled to God through Christ's death (the veil of flesh He passed through). His resurrection life in us is what saves. So we see here that atonement is not yet salvation. It is the prerequisite and seal of assurance that we will arrive.

Paul wrote to the Ephesians: "...having believed, you were sealed with the Holy Spirit of promise, who is the guarantee of our inheritance until the redemption of the purchased possession" (Eph. 1:13-4). The word translated as redemption in this passage is *apolutrosis* (629). It means "to be purchased from the slave market of sin, totally set free, never to be sold again". So when believers sing, "I've been redeemed by the blood of the Lamb", redemption refers to a future event. Blood is the eternal life of the Holy Spirit that guarantees it. We have been purchased, sealed, and will eventually be totally set free.

MacDonald said that many people are content with the assurance of salvation, but do not want salvation itself. In other words, they want a guarantee of Paradise, a place they call heaven, a place where there is no suffering. But they do not want to rid themselves of the sin that causes suffering. They do not want to work out their own salvation. (Phil. 2:12). So, what does Paul mean when he says we are not saved by works, lest anyone should boast (Eph. 2:8-9)? How can we then work out our own salvation?

The following passage about how faith, not works, is related to salvation is often isolated from other Scripture. Therefore, it has been misunderstood as supporting a vicarious or penal substitution paradigm. The context of Scripture is the Bible in its entirety. If an interpretation is correct, all passages will integrate rationally. Paul wrote to the Romans a passage that included a quote from Genesis:

> What then shall we say that Abraham our father has found according to the flesh? For if Abraham was justified by works, he has *something* to boast about, but not before God. For what does the Scripture say? "Abraham believed God, and it was accounted to him for righteousness" [Gen. 15:6]. Now to him who works, the wages are not counted as grace but as debt. But to him who does not work but believes on Him who justifies the ungodly, his faith is accounted for righteousness… (Rom. 4:1-5).

Abraham's faith was accounted to him as righteousness. Faith and righteousness are spiritual attributes. Work and wages are physical references. Once again Paul is trying to lift his audience's understanding above the physical into the spiritual domain. Spiritual virtues cannot be earned through physical labor. This passage from *Romans* states that God did not acknowledge works, which in context referred to adherence to the Jewish law of circumcision. The point of the passage was that Abraham was pronounced righteous prior to the covenant of circumcision and Law of Moses. If he was righteous before the law of circumcision, it would obviously not be the work of circumcision that accomplished his righteousness.

There are different types of works, and James felt the necessity to clarify the distinction by affirming some works do, in fact, *justify*.

> But do you want to know, O foolish man, that faith without works is dead? Was not Abraham our father justified by works when he offered Isaac his son on the altar? Do you see that faith was working together with his works, and by works faith was made perfect? And the Scripture was fulfilled which says, "Abraham believed God, and it was accounted to him for righteousness." And he was called the friend of God. You see then that a man is justified by works, and not by faith only (Jam. 2:20-4).

Paul was addressing the culture of a people who accepted the testimony of Christ, but were reluctant to let go of Mosaic traditions. Christian Jews wanted Gentile converts to be circumcised and follow their customs. Paul was trying to explain to them that the works of the Old Testament ordinances and rituals could not justify (correct, align) our conscience (thoughts and awareness) with God. The law was instituted for its metaphoric, prophetic, and social benefit.

The value of circumcision was in its symbolic meaning. It could not make a man inwardly good to save him from his sins. Our physical actions are merely a reflection of our hearts and minds. Isolating Paul's teachings from the passage in James can lead to confusion. Are we saved by works, or not?

When discussing the concept of works, motivation is the distinguishing factor. Heaven is not the reward of virtue. Heaven is the result. If one's motivation is reward, works cannot save. When love of God (truth, righteousness, mercy) is the motivation, that is salvation itself. God is the believer's inheritance. Righteousness is its own reward. The Christian life is not measured by what a man did or did not do; it is measured by what a man becomes. Treasures of heaven are virtues not selfish desires.

St. Clement of Alexandria refers to an interesting saying, but fails to cite its source, probably because the quote was well known at the time. I am convinced it must have been passed down by verbal tradition among early believers, because I have read it elsewhere in my readings of the early saints. The quote is this, "For by the state in which I find you will I judge" (*Selected Works*, 735). I believe this, and it is supported by Scripture (Eze. 18:21-4).

Abraham's faith in God, His truth, righteousness, mercy and sovereignty, produced works of obedience that justified (aligned) him with God's purposes; and that was held to be righteousness. As James pointed out, his faith was not *perfect* (*teleioo*, meaning *complete*) until he acted on it. God did not simply substitute someone else's righteousness for Abraham's, and there is no record that the patriarch believed He would.

Abraham's saving faith was not in a God Who required a propitiatory sacrifice to appease His anger. His faith was clearly not in a vicarious substitutionary sacrifice. The sin offering had not yet been established. Abraham's faith was in the belief that God would fulfill His promise of a coming Messiah through Isaac's bloodline (Heb. 11:17-8). The writer of *Hebrews* continues, "...concluding that God *was* able to raise *him* up, even from the dead" (Heb. 11:19).

The event, recorded in Genesis 22, was a foreshadowing of a future time when God would provide His only Son as a sacrifice for us. Walking up the mount with wood, knife, and fire, Isaac asked his father where the lamb was for the sacrifice. Abraham prophetically answered, "My son, God will provide Himself a lamb for the burnt offering" (Gen. 22:8, KJV). He trusted in God's provision.

As with all Scripture, there is a symbolic portrayal of Christ and/or spiritual reality. The prophetic lesson of that incident would not be fully understood until the time of the crucifixion. The point is this event was not a lesson in the necessity of propitiating Divine wrath with death. This story does not imply that. As Abraham raised his knife over his son on the altar, God stopped him, "Do not lay your hand on the lad, or do anything to him; for now I know that you fear God, since you have not withheld your son, your only *son*, from Me" (Gen. 22:12).

The word translated *fear* in this passage is *yare*. It means reverencing, which is to have deep respect, high regard or admiration, an intense adoring awed respect. This is not the type of fear that produces compliance through force of power. It is awe produced by the nature of His being, which is love, truth, righteousness, mercy and so forth. It is not a power that extorts submission. It is a nature that elicits desire.

Abraham's righteous faith stemmed from his love of God. The passage states, he was a friend of God. His knowledge of God's nature gave him confidence that He knows what is best, asks what's right, and has purposes we cannot see. Abraham's faith in God's goodness was his righteousness. The righteousness of Christ, which Paul speaks of having, is real righteousness not a vicarious one. That righteousness is truth, love, mercy, and trust oriented, as opposed to law, ritual, and punishment oriented.

In the book of *Samuel,* Saul was chastised and disciplined when he disobeyed God's command and tried to establish his own righteousness:

And Saul said to Samuel, "But I have obeyed the voice of the LORD, and gone on the mission on which the LORD sent me, and brought back Agag king of Amalek; I have utterly destroyed the Amalekites. But the people took of the plunder, sheep and oxen, the best of the things which should have been destroyed, to sacrifice to the LORD your God in Gilgal". So Samuel said: "Has the LORD *as great* delight in burnt offerings and sacrifices, as in obeying the voice of the LORD? Behold, to obey is better than sacrifice, *and* to heed than the fat of rams. For rebellion *is as* the sin of witchcraft, and stubbornness *is as* iniquity

and idolatry. Because you have rejected the word of the
LORD, He also has rejected you from being king" (I Sam.
15:20-3).

Saul disobeyed God by keeping some of the plundered
livestock for sacrifice, instead of destroying them as
commanded. In this case, what Saul thought would be a good
work approved by God, worked against him. Frequently
throughout the Old Testament, God reprimands His people
for substituting sacrifices for obedience.

Jeremiah prophesied:

> For I did not speak to your fathers or command them the
> day I brought them out of Egypt, concerning burnt
> offerings or sacrifices. But this is what I commanded
> them saying, "Obey my voice and I will be your God and
> you shall be my people…" (Jer. 7:22-3).

The Hebrew system of sacrifice was established later as a
prophetic identifier of the promised Messiah. Saul could not
have simply offered a sacrifice to substitute and eliminate the
consequences of his disobedience.

Scripture teaches we cannot ignore what we are told to do
and then later hope to make up for it by doing some other
good work of our choosing. Good works, those done at a
convenient time or out of a guilty conscience, will not save
us. Our independent plans, no matter how well intentioned,
will not unite us with the Father in Christ and His universal
plan for redemption. We must be partakers of His Divine plan
by faith, as Abraham was. That is the saving faith Paul is
addressing.

Eternal life is to know God (John 17:3). To know God is
to hear God. Jesus said, "My sheep hear My voice, and I
know them, and they follow Me" (John 10:27).

John writes about a group of people who followed Jesus
after they were fed when He multiplied the five loaves and
two fish. "Then they said to Him, 'What shall we do that we

may work the works of God?' Jesus answered and said, to them, 'This is the work of God, that you believe in Him whom He sent'" (John 6:28-9). God's "work" is to believe in The Word of God incarnate, for believing in the Word means acting in trust on what we have been told by Christ. To move in faith can indeed be hard work, especially when it goes against our reasoning. Just like Abraham, our actions, not our words, reflect the depth of our beliefs.

Jesus said, "Not everyone who says to me, 'Lord, Lord,' shall enter the kingdom of heaven, but he who does the will of My Father in heaven" (Matt. 7:21). The will of the Father is that we trust the teachings of His Son. Simple enough. Begin now by doing the next thing at hand that Jesus instructed. If you don't know, start with the sermon on the mount.

Note that obedience is not perfection. It is simply trying. What parent is not pleased with their child's first attempts at addition? Yet, who would be satisfied if they did not advance to multiplication? We have all missed the mark, as the bull's eye is not hit in the first endeavor. But what parent is not pleased with their child's willingness?

There are many judgments along the way and everyone will stand before the judgment seat of God. Paul wrote in *Romans*:

> But in accordance with your hardness and your impenitent heart you are treasuring up for yourself wrath in the day of wrath and revelation of the righteous judgment of God, who "will render to each one according to his deeds": eternal life to those who by patient continuance in doing good seek for glory, honor, and immortality; but to those who are self-seeking and do not obey the truth, but obey unrighteousness—indignation and wrath, tribulation and anguish, on every soul of man who does evil, of the Jew first and also of the Greek; but glory, honor, and peace to everyone who works what is good, to the Jew first and also to the Greek (Rom. 2:5-9).

Note that there is no mention that God's wrath will be unending. Although Scripture indicates that our actions resonate in the eternal, God promises the reconciliation of all things. That restoration will be elaborated upon in the next chapter.

Regarding judgment, Jesus said, "For the Father judges no one, but has committed all judgment to the Son" (John 5:22). Yet, a few chapters later in the same gospel Jesus said:

And if anyone hears My words and does not believe, I do not judge him; for I did not come to judge the world but to save the world. He who rejects Me, and does not receive My words, has that which judges him—the word that I have spoken will judge him in the last day... (John 12:47-8).

The same message is reiterated in the parable of the wise man building his house on the rock and the foolish man on the sand (Matt. 7:24-29). The outcome in the day of revelation will itself be the judge. Adam and Eve could never have foreseen the extended horrific outcome of their lack of trusting God. It left the entire world and all their progeny in a critical condition of disorientation and moral decay.

The writer of *Hebrews* asks the question, "How shall we escape if we neglect so great a salvation?" (Heb. 2:3). He was referencing neglecting the words spoken by Christ, not the affirmation of an obscure paradigm on how atonement works devised centuries after His death. John explains why men are condemned to disorientation and suffering, "And this is the condemnation, that the light has come into the world, and men loved darkness rather than light, because their deeds were evil" (John 3:19).

God grieves over the repercussions of neglecting His Word. Jesus lamented over the inescapable consequences Jerusalem would face as a result of rejecting His guidance.

Now as He drew near, He saw the city and wept over it, saying, "If you had known, even you, especially in this your day, the things *that make* for your peace! But now they are hidden from your eyes" (Luke 19:41-2).

Sin and selfish desire cloud truth. Many of the Jews wanted to believe in a redeemer that would physically free them from Roman rule. The utter destruction of Jerusalem would follow several years after the rejection of Jesus as the true Messiah and His revelation of the things that make for peace.

In His grief, Jesus foretold the details:

For the days will come upon you when your enemies will build an embankment around you surround you and close you in on every side, and level you, and your children within you, to the ground; and they will not leave in you one stone upon another… (Luke 19:43-4).

In 70 A.D. armies of the Roman Emperor Titus would lay siege to Jerusalem. The Roman army would burn the city and level it, literally leaving it with not "one stone upon another". Thus the abundant amount of gold in the temple and elsewhere, which melted from the fire, could be pillaged. However, the words Christ used to explain what was bringing Him to anguish were that the people would not accept "the things that make for peace". They wanted a physical freedom from Roman rule, not a spiritual kingdom where the humble servant is deemed the greatest. They heard what they wanted to hear; consequently, the truth of the eternal gospel was eclipsed, and they could not be saved from the wrath that was to come.

Many of those who rejected Jesus embraced false Messiahs. Prominent among the pseudo saviors at that time were the Zealots, who gained power by promising freedom from Roman oppression. Their rebellion resulted in the fulfillment of Christ's prophecy concerning Jerusalem. Those who believed Christ, and obeyed, were saved from the brutal siege tactics and wrath of the Zealots and Titus. They were able to flee the city at the forewarned time (Mat. 24:15-8).

Another passage cited to support atonement by vicarious substitution uses the word *propitiation,* which has been construed to mean the Father was being appeased by Christ's death. But Paul wrote that we, not God, needed propitiating. "And you, who once were alienated and enemies in your mind by wicked works, yet now He has reconciled in the body of His flesh through death..." (Col 1:21). Is it believable that God, who is all-powerful, all-knowing, all-loving, and all-wise—the Designer and Creator of all things—needs to be propitiated? Furthermore, an offering is intended to reconcile the receiver, not the giver.

Scripture does not say that God was appeasing Himself by His own sacrifice. In the following passage, note that Christ was set forth (presented or displayed) as a peace offering given <u>to us</u>. The Father sent Jesus to reveal the truth of His welcoming heart, and the gift of His Holy Spirit.

> Now the righteousness of God apart from the law is revealed, being witnessed by the Law and the Prophets, even the righteousness of God through faith in Jesus Christ, to all and on all who believe. For there is no difference; for all have sinned and fall short of the glory of God, being justified freely by His grace through the redemption that is in Christ Jesus, whom God <u>set forth as a propitiation</u> by His blood, through faith, to demonstrate His righteousness, because in His forbearance God had passed over the sins that were previously committed, to demonstrate at the present time His righteousness, that He might be just and the justifier of the one who has faith in Jesus (Rom. 3:21-6).

The word propitiation in that passage is a translation from the Greek word *hilasterion,* which is literally rendered *a mercy seat* or *mercy establishment.* So the underlined phrase from the last passage is literally translated "whom God set forth as a mercy seat by His blood (life)".

What is the mercy seat? The Hebrew word is *kapporeth,* which means to *cover, wipe out or cleanse.* It was the cover, which rested over the Ark of the Covenant. The Ark contained the *testimony* (Ex. 25:16), the Old Testament Commandments from God. So, the law was covered by the mercy seat, a golden lid with two seraphim (angels) at either side. Their wings covered the seat. The law was symbolically covered, wiped out or cleansed by mercy.

Once a year on the Day of Atonement, the blood of an animal without spot or blemish, representing the life of a sinless offering, was sprinkled on the mercy seat. It was sprinkled first for the High Priest and then for the people. This blood represented the Holy Spirit (Heb. 9:7-8).

The blood (life) shed by Christ is the Eternal Life that washes us from sin. We are washed in His life. These are transcendent realities represented by physical analogies. What other reality can John be speaking of when he writes: "Unto him that loved us, and washed us from our sins in his own blood" (Rev. 1:5). A literal interpretation is illogical as physical blood is anything but cleansing. A vicarious washing is not reality based.

As demonstrated in the completed historical context (see Chapter 5), it is not death that propitiates or makes amends, but the righteous life (blood) that is sprinkled on the mercy seat. Cleansing and life, not death, is the context. The eternal life in Christ was set forth, eternal life was demonstrated, eternal life alone can justify, correct, reconcile/propitiate, resurrect.

The death of Jesus was not a compensation to satisfy some philosophical principle of justice taught by legalists and denounced by Him. His death was the means to the offering of Divine life. He "ascended far above all the heavens, that He might fill all things" (Eph. 4:10). With what? Divine Life. "And this is the record, that God has given to us eternal life, and this life is in his Son" (I John 5:11). This life in the Son is

His Word and Spirit. He had to pass through the veil of human flesh, and thus death, to offer this gift. Jesus, the fulfillment of the Levitical priest offering for sins of ignorance brought us the knowledge of God and the free gift of Divine eternal life for all who receive and have faith in His Word and Spirit.

The cross was a consequence of shining light into dark, narcissistic lives. Christ's righteousness was threatening to many because He claimed He would establish a new kingdom order. This new order is one in which the power structure of this world—money, beauty, intelligence, athletic abilities, religious position, etc.—are all replaced. The priorities of worldly values are reversed in the new kingdom order.

Jesus said, "But many *who are* first will be last, and the last first" (Matt. 19:30). Later He added, "But he who is greatest among you shall be your servant. And whoever exalts himself will be humbled, and he who humbles himself will be exalted" (Matt. 23:11-2). This is a threatening reversal of fortune, indeed, for those who seek to prosper in this current life by aspiring to power and authority. Jesus justified His words with His action. He did not strike back at His persecutors, yet He was victorious through the resurrection.

Thus, the reasons for Christ's death: "Unless a grain of wheat falls into the ground and dies, it remains alone; but if it dies it produces much grain. He who loves his life will lose it, and he who hates his life in this world will keep it for eternal life" (John 12:24-5). "And I, if I am lifted up from the earth, will draw all men unto Me" (John 12:32, KJV). We are drawn to Christ if for no other reason than to try to comprehend the strength of love. His sacrifice stretches far beyond our capacity to comprehend it cognitively. We must move beyond ourselves and touch the Divine to fathom the depth of it.

Paul elaborates on the meaning of Christ's reconciliation in the *Second Epistle to the Corinthians*. "For He made Him who knew no sin to be sin for us, that we might become the righteousness of God in Him" (II Cor. 5:21). A literal rendering of this passage makes no sense, because sin is an action. So, how is it to be understood? It implies that the Word of God took on the same sin nature that we have, by becoming a physical man.

Paul's clarification is found in *Romans*. "For what the law could not do, in that it was weak through the flesh, God sending his own Son in the likeness of sinful flesh, and for sin, condemned sin in the flesh" (Rom. 8:3). Christ overcame the sinful nature of the flesh, thus condemning it. Christ bore with us our burden of sin by allowing Himself to be treated like a sinner in taking on Adam's DNA. That experience included physical death, which we will all face. Jesus became our older brother, mediating between the Father and us (Heb. 2:11).

Our righteousness is not Christ's righteousness being substituted for our unrighteousness. It is rather that "we might become the righteousness of God in Him". I have been told that Christ gave us the Sermon on the Mount just to show us that we could not live up to the righteousness required by God for salvation. That begs the question, why then did Jesus tell his disciples to go into all nations, make disciples, "teaching them to observe all things that I have commanded you" (Matt. 28:20), rather than teaching them to trust in His finished work?

Who would tell their child, you will never be capable of running a marathon, but I want you to train for it? You will never have the strength to finish and obtain the prize, but make it your highest calling. Where would the hope and joy be in that? What rational man, woman, or child would take the effort seriously when everyone receives the same prize of vicarious virtue in the end? Why would Jesus tell us to strive for something we could receive without effort?

The commandments Christ gave us are spiritual. Paul chided the Galatians by asking, "Having begun in the Spirit, are you now being made perfect by the flesh?" (Gal. 3:3). He was telling them that fleshly perfection by Mosaic standards could not save them. It will fall short. "You have heard it said to those of old, 'You shall not murder ...' "But I say to you that whoever is angry…" (Matt. 5:21). So we see how mere physical compliance cannot finish the race. Simply not killing your brother is not enough. It is the condition of your heart.

Paul writes to the Philippians, "For it is God who works in you both to will and to do for *His* good pleasure" (Phil. 2:13). There are legions of unholy spirits working in our world causing pain and suffering. God's Holy Spirit works in us to comfort, guide, inform us of spiritual realities, and lead us into all truth. But as Paul wrote, "…you are that one's slaves whom you obey, whether of sin unto death, or of obedience unto righteousness" (Rom. 6:16, KJV).

In summary, redemption is a multifaceted process that begins with accepting Jesus as Lord and Savior. Just as earthly parents love, forgive, nurture and help their children grow into adulthood, so does our Spiritual Father. But His love extends far beyond what we can grasp on our own.

God sends us His light through Jesus Christ and the Holy Spirit. Sometimes light shows the way, sometimes it warms, sometimes it burns. It always reveals and purifies. "He who has begun a good work in you will complete it…" (Phil. 1:6). Our union with the Father through the Son saves us. The affirming of doctrinal creeds and paradigms cannot save. One of the main tenets of Martin Luther's Protestant Reformation was that salvation is by faith, not by intellectual assent to doctrine.

But what if that *good work* was never begun in one's lifetime? What if one's life is lived in complete hostility toward God? What if someone never heard the gospel? Can death close the door to all hope for them?

Chapter 7

Reconciliation & Restoration: All or Some?

Who then can be saved? The Apostles asked Jesus that question after He had said, "It is easier for a camel to go through the eye of a needle than for a rich man to enter the kingdom of God". His answer: "With men this is impossible, but with God all things are possible" (Matt. 19:24, 26). If you are rich, take heart, God can still save you. God can save all.

American essayist Logan Pearsall Smith once quipped, "It is the wretchedness of being rich that you have to live with rich people". Some people can be so absorbed in a materialistic lifestyle they neglect spiritual values. So, the implicit message of Christ's statement about the difficulty of a rich man entering the kingdom of God is that some people may be harder to save than others. But that passage reassures us that "with God all things are possible".

The Apostle Peter preached perhaps the most unambiguous message of God's universal reconciliation: "… until the times of restoration of all things, which God has spoken by the mouth of all His holy prophets since the world began" (Acts 3:21). Peter also wrote, "The Lord is not slack concerning His promise, as some count slackness, but is longsuffering toward us, not willing that any should perish but that all should come to repentance" (II Pet. 3:9). Paul exhorted Timothy to pray for "all men, for kings and all who are in authority that we may lead a quiet and peaceable life in all godliness and reverence; for this *is* good and acceptable in the sight of God our Savior, who desires all men to be saved and to come to the knowledge of the truth" (I Tim. 2:1-4).

Those who believe God predestines some for heaven and some for hell have maintained that God does not actually desire that all should be saved. After all, if He is able to save all and does not, He must not want to. They say *all* only represents all of a certain group. Once again, to say God is of such character is "as loathsome a lie against God as could find place in the heart too undeveloped to understand what justice is, and too low to look up into the face of Jesus".

God "works all things according to the counsel of His will" (Eph. 1:11). So, God's promise, "the restoration of all things"; and desire, for "all men to be saved and to come to the knowledge of the truth"; plus God's ability, "with God all things are possible"; equals God's action, "all shall be made alive". Paul wrote to the Corinthians, "For as in Adam all die, even so in Christ all shall be made alive. But each one in his own order: Christ the firstfruits, afterward those *who* are Christ's at His coming" (I Cor. 15:22-3).

That is often interpreted *all in Christ* rather than *in Christ all* shall be saved, rendering the passage to mean that those who are outside of Christ will not be gathered in Him. But the verse does not say that. It plainly says, "...in Christ <u>all</u> shall be made alive". That is the same *all* as those who are dead in Adam—everyone.

The passage then goes on to clarify not who will be saved (made alive in Christ), but rather in what order they will be saved. Next to the foundational teachings of Christ, this Scripture is key because it is so straightforward and unambiguous that it cannot mean anything else. It must be removed, totally ignored, or believed. If it is believed, it must be foundational, due to its simplicity. Of course this creates the necessity to take a more comprehensive look at other passages that have been interpreted as contradicting its assertion. That is obviously what this book is about.

That same message is repeated in *Romans*, "For God has committed them all to disobedience, that He might have mercy on all" (Rom. 11:32). God will have mercy on everyone who is disobedient. But who are the disobedient? "God has committed them all to disobedience". So on whom will God have mercy? Everyone. He is a Father who loves all His creation, even though they are all committed to disobedience.

Also, we are told God's mercy will last forever. The following verse is cited twice in the Old Testament: "Oh, give thanks to the LORD, for *He is* good! For His mercy *endures* forever" (Psa. 118:1 & I Chr. 16:34). Since God's mercy endures forever, it would be illogical to assume anyone could pass beyond it. Those who argue that His mercy endures forever for a chosen few only need to reread Romans 11:32. He will have mercy on all.

When John the Baptist first saw Jesus walking toward him, he said, "Behold! The Lamb of God who takes away the sin of the world!" (John 1:29). John did not say, "The Lamb of God who takes away the sin of the elect, the chosen, the predestined few, or even those who believe He takes away their sin". He said, "The Lamb of God who takes away the sin of the world".

Some people argue that Jesus took away all sin, but a person must receive the gift of forgiveness, and many people do not choose to accept that gift. Therefore, those people's sins are never taken away. But forgiveness does not take away sin; it can only help reconcile its affects. Again, sin is an action. Sin is only taken away when people cease to engage in it. Since the quote specifically says "the sin of the world", that leaves two conclusions: either (1) all men will eventually be cleansed of their leanings toward sin in this life or the next, or (2) Jesus will only effectively take away some of the sins of the world. If that was the case, John could just as easily have said, the Lamb of God who takes away the sins of the chosen few, which is what many theologians teach.

Jesus did say, "For many are called but few chosen". That begs the question, chosen for what? The answer cannot be chosen for salvation in Christ without contradicting other Scripture. That statement concludes the parable of the laborers in the vineyard. What is the context and point of the story? The employer paid those he hired at the end of the day the same wages he paid those who worked the whole day, and the laborers who worked longer complained. To make matters worse, those who were hired near the end of the day were paid first. The story closes with, "So the last will be first, and the first last. For many are called but few chosen" (Matt. 20:16). The implication is that all receive, but some (the elect) are chosen to receive first. The context is about the chosen order. After all, both first and last received their wages.

Jesus said, "Now is the judgment of this world; now the ruler of this world will be cast out, and I, if I am lifted up from the earth, will draw all *men* unto Me" (John 12:31-2). All will be drawn to Christ, but will all receive salvation? Paul wrote, "Therefore, as through one man's offense [Adam] *judgment* came to all men, resulting in condemnation, even so through one Man's righteous act [Jesus] *the free gift came* to all men, resulting in justification of life" (Rom. 5:18). The same all who are condemned are justified. The correlation is unmistakably obvious in the *Greek Interlinear Bible*: "So then as through one deviation to all men to condemnation, so also through one righteous act to all men to justification".

The message is clear. Scripture repeats it multiple times in multiple ways. The only way that the meaning of these passages cannot be heard is if they are interpreted through a presupposition filtering out that message.

The theme that Christ will draw all men unto Himself and take away their sins is presented throughout the Bible. This message can only be mistaken if passages are taken out of context or interpreted outside their cultural and historical frame of reference.

This passage from *Romans* sheds light on that promise, even though it only references one group of people.

And so all Israel will be saved, as it is written: "The Deliverer will come out of Zion, and He will turn away ungodliness from Jacob; for this is My covenant with them, when I take away their sins" (Rom. 11:26-7).

Some have argued that this passage refers to *spiritual Israel*, those who have faith in the same promise, of Jesus the Messiah, as Abraham did (Rom. 9:7-8). They contend all of Abraham's genetic descendants could not possibly be redeemed because many of them died without believing in Jesus the Messiah, and they believe there is no salvation after death.

However, look at the passage in context. This entire chapter in *Romans* talks about how Israel rejected the gospel so that it would be taken to the Gentiles. In the context of the chapter, Israel is no more spiritual Israel than the Gentiles are spiritual Gentiles. The Scripture says specifically "all Israel will be saved".

How are we to come to grips with the statement that all Israel will be saved? It is through recognizing that not only all of Israel but the entire world will be saved. Paul wrote, "For if their [the Jews] being cast away *is* the reconciling of the world, what *will* their acceptance be but life from the dead?" (Rom. 11:15).

Consider again this passage from *II Corinthians*:

Now all things are of God, who has reconciled us to Himself through Jesus Christ, and has given us the ministry of reconciliation, that is, that God was in Christ reconciling the world to Himself, not imputing their trespasses to them, and has committed to us the word of reconciliation (II Cor. 5:18-9).

This Scripture does not say God was reconciling "some of the world" to Himself. It says "the world". It says God was not imputing our trespasses to us. This passage unequivocally communicates good news for everyone.

Again, Paul wrote to the church in Ephesus:

…making known to us the mystery of His will, according to His good pleasure which He purposed in Himself, for the administration of the fullness of the times to head up all things in Christ, both the things in the heavens and the things on earth—in Him (Eph. 1:9-10 Literal Greek trans.)

Some argue that which is in hell will not be gathered, reconciled or restored in Him. But as demonstrated in Chapter 2, the Biblical words for hell (the Hebrew word *Sheol* and the Greek word *Hades*) literally mean "the unseen state". Since the physical is ever changing and destined to completely perish, but not the eternal unseen state, the gathering must especially include *Hades* or *Sheol*.

Paul's letter to the *Colossians* presents the most unequivocal explanation of this reality in Christ:

He [Christ] is the image of the invisible God, the firstborn over all creation. For by Him all things were created that are in heaven and that are on earth, visible and invisible, whether thrones or dominions or principalities or powers. All things were created through Him and for Him. And He is before all things, and in Him all things consist. And He is the head of the body, the church, who is the beginning, the firstborn from the dead, that in all things He may have the preeminence. For it pleased *the Father that* in Him all the fullness should dwell, and by Him to reconcile all things to Himself, by Him, whether things on earth or things in heaven, having made peace through the blood of His cross. And you, who once were alienated and enemies in your mind by wicked works, yet now He has reconciled in the body of His flesh through death, to present you holy, and blameless, and above reproach in His sight (Col. 1:15-22).

Note how the repeated parallel structure of this passage makes perfectly clear that "all" created things is the same "all" as that which will be reconciled. All things are created through the Son, for the Son, consist in the Son, and will be reconciled to the Son by the Son.

According to *Strong's Concordance*, to *reconcile all things* means to change fully from one condition to another, so as to remove all enmity and leave no impediment to unity and peace (#604, *apokatallasso*). Being tormented apart from God without end would seem to me an "impediment to unity".

In *James* we read, "Of His own will, He brought forth by the word of truth, that we might be a kind of firstfruits of His creatures" (Jam. 1:18). James was describing the believers who were alive at the time of his writing as firstfruits. So, where does that place people who had died before James? More to the point, since we know there are firstfruits, doesn't that make you wonder who are the secondfruits? And the thirdfruits? The fact is, we have no idea in what order people are saved. However, we do know that physical death cannot be the end of the reconciliation process since we are told throughout Scripture that God will reconcile, not some, but all things in His order.

Also, the passage from *Peter*, cited in Chapter 3, referenced Christ preaching after His death to those who had died in the days of Noah, thousands of years earlier. That passage presents the idea that Christ is always continuously working to reconcile all sinners, even those who had physically died.

Paul wrote in *Philippians*:

Therefore God also has highly exalted Him and given Him the name which is above every name, that at the name of Jesus every knee should bow, of those in heaven, and those on earth, and of those under the earth, and *that* every tongue should confess that Jesus Christ is Lord, to the glory of God the Father (Phil. 2:9-11).

Confession is the specific act about which Paul wrote to the *Romans* that all people must do to be saved. "If you confess with your mouth the Lord Jesus and believe in your heart that God has raised Him from the dead, you will be saved" (Rom. 10:9). Then Paul goes on to quote from the Old Testament prophet Joel: "Whoever calls on the name of the Lord shall be saved" (Joel 2:32).

The Scriptural references to kneeling down before the Lord refer back to a prophecy in *Isaiah*:

Look to Me, and be saved, all you ends of the earth! For I *am* God, and *there is* no other. I have sworn by Myself; the word has gone out of My mouth *in* righteousness, and shall not return, that to me every knee shall bow, every tongue shall take an oath. He shall say, "Surely in the LORD I have righteousness and strength. To Him *men* shall come, and all shall be ashamed who are incensed against Him" (Isa. 45:22-4).

Every knee will bow and every tongue will confess. But confess what? "Surely in the Lord I have righteousness and strength". That certainly does not sound like a forced confession. Where would be the logic in the God of Truth coercing a lie out of people? The Divine Spirit can only be worshipped in sincerity (John 4:24), and worship requires a humble reverence. God does not care for feigned honor or obeisance. How are all those incensed against Him to be ashamed when intimidation tends to foster resentment? No one likes to be terrorized. Terror may produce fear but certainly not shame. This passage clearly does not imply force.

So how does the rider on the white horse (Jesus) called Faithful and True judge and make war? (Rev. 19:11) It is the Word of God, the sword, proceeding from His mouth that smites the nations and conquers. "For the word of God is living and powerful, and sharper than any two-edged sword, piercing even to the division of soul and spirit, and of joints and marrow, and is a discerner of the thoughts and intents of the heart" (Heb. 4: 12).

The rod of iron is symbolic language used by Isaiah as "the rod of His mouth". (Isa. 11: 4). Jesus said "Heaven and earth will pass away, but My words will by no means pass away" (Matt. 24: 35). His words will be like a rod of iron, unbending. The consequences, of keeping or not keeping the commandments of Christ, have and will always be the ultimate judge. It will correct us; it will smite us or reward us.

The question is: Did we build our lives on truth or lies, on solid rock or shifting sand? Jesus said:

> I have come *as* a light into the world, that whoever believes in Me should not abide in darkness. And if anyone hears My words and does not believe, I do not judge him; for I did not come to judge the world but to save the world. He who rejects Me, and does not receive My words, has that which judges him- the word that I have spoken will judge him in the last day. For I have not spoken on My own *authority*; but the Father who sent Me gave Me a command, what I should say and what I should speak (John 12:46-9).

In His Sermon on the Mount Jesus concluded by saying that those who would not follow His guidance would suffer the type of consequences that a foolish man building his house on sand would suffer. The house would fall and great would be the fall of it (Matt. 7:26-7). Have we not watched this reality played out in the rise and fall of nation after nation? How shall we escape if we neglect so great a salvation, which at the first began to be spoken by the Lord?" (Heb.2:3).

Many of us are slow learners but our Heavenly Father is patient. Who can resist real love forever? Love is the most powerful force in the universe. It will liberate from the desire to dominate, freeing us to embrace compassionate service as Jesus taught and modeled? When blameless and upright Job finally comes face to face with God, he responds, "I have heard of You by the hearing of the ear. But now my eye sees You. Therefore I abhor *myself*, and repent in dust and ashes" (Job 42:5-6). Omnipotence may terrorize and shrink one to a groveling slave; however, it was the nature, not the power of God that reduced Job to awe, repentance and worship. Job's spiritual revelation led him to see himself more clearly and to abhor what he saw.

There can be no more need in the Divine Love to extract feigned reverence from us than healthy parents need to extract veneration from their infants. Spiritual worship is essential to our well-being because it connects us to our eternal life source. Although God is worthy, God does not need our worship!

Adam's descendants will eventually come to authentic devotion through experience, like Job. In the last chapter of *Revelation* John writes: "He who is unjust, let him be unjust still; he who is filthy, let him be filthy still..." (Rev. 22:11). Why would such a decree be given when throughout Scripture we are admonished to repent and live righteously? The prophet Jeremiah gave us the answer, "Your own wickedness will correct you, and your backslidings will rebuke you..." (Jer. 2:19a). God's love is a patient, irresistible force.

Francis Thompson penned these words about God's persistent pursuit in his famous poem *The Hound of Heaven*:

> I fled Him down the nights and down the days,
> I fled Him, down the arches of the years,
> I fled Him, down the labyrinthine ways,
> Of my own mind; and in the mist of tears,
> I hid from Him, and under running laughter,
> Up vistaed hopes I sped,
> And shot, precipitated,
> Adown Titanic glooms of chasmed fears,
> From those strong Feet that followed, followed after,
> But with unhurrying chase,
> And unperturbed pace,
> Deliberate speed, majestic instancy,

> They beat—and a Voice beat
> More instant than the Feet—
> "All things betray thee, who betrayest Me".

Experience will teach that everything but the love and truth of God betrays. Men who love darkness and evil invite the outer darkness and the consuming fire of God's love.

George MacDonald wrote:

> God in the dark can make a man thirst for the light, who never in the light sought but the dark.... Unfelt, unprized, the light must be taken from him, that he may know what the darkness is (*Creation in Christ*, 172).

The good news is that the eternal fire and darkness are redeeming simply because God's devotion will not be satisfied with anything less than salvation for all from sin.

Nothing but the eternal presence of the Father can satisfy our deepest needs because we are made in His image. Jesus promised, if we seek God with all our heart we will find Him:

> Ask, and it will be given to you; seek, and you will find; knock, and it will be opened to you. For everyone who asks receives, and he who seeks finds, and to him who knocks it will be opened. If a son asks for bread from any father among you, will he give him a stone? Or if he asks for a fish, will he give him a serpent instead of a fish? Or if he asks for an egg, will he offer him a scorpion? If you then, being evil, know how to give good gifts to your children, how much more will your heavenly Father give the Holy Spirit to those who ask Him! (Luke 11:9-13).

In *Matthew*, Jesus reiterated:

> Come to Me, all *you* who labor and are heavy laden, and I will give you rest. Take My yoke upon you and learn from Me, for I am gentle and lowly in heart and you will

find rest for your souls. For My yoke *is* easy and My burden is light (Matt. 11:28-30).

If Christ is the image of the invisible God and He is gentle and lowly in heart, then so is the Father.

The prophet Isaiah declared:

He will swallow up death forever, and the Lord GOD will wipe away tears from all faces; the rebuke of His people He will take away from all the earth; for the Lord has spoken. And it will be said in that day: "Behold, this *is* our God; we have waited for Him, and He will save us. This *is* the LORD; we have waited for Him; we will be glad and rejoice in His salvation" (Isa. 25:8-9).

Since this passage states "God will wipe away the tears from all faces", that begs the question how He could do that for those burning in everlasting torment. The prophecy goes on to explain how. He will take away the *rebuke*, that is the disgrace, from all the earth, and "He will save us". His life will swallow up death!

Some commentators have stated the word *all* in that passage does not really mean everyone. They point out that *all* can be used metaphorically or as hyperbole, as in phrases like "in all honesty" or "all roads lead to Rome". However, in the two verses prior to this passage, *all* is used three other times and in each case means everyone. If we apply standard hermeneutical methods to this passage by using the Bible to interpret the Bible, it can only mean everyone.

Paul instructed Timothy to be diligent in preaching the gospel, "For this *end* we both labor and suffer reproach, because we trust in the living God, who is the Savior of all men, especially of those who believe" (I Tim. 4:10). How can Christ be the Savior of all and *especially* the Savior of some? This verse specifically says God saves everyone and emphasizes those who are believers. Why? Because salvation is a process and believers are closer to the end. Being conformed into the image of Christ is our salvation.

The Scripture does not say Christ is *potentially* the Savior of all. It says He is "the Savior of all". This verse would be contradictory or unintelligible unless we accept that some people are specifically being saved now, that is the elect; but eventually all will be reconciled and saved.

Speaking of the *Son of Man*, as Jesus frequently referred to Himself, *Daniel* prophesied: "And to him is given dominion, and glory, and a kingdom, and all peoples, nations, and languages do serve him, his dominion is a dominion age-during, that passes not away, and his kingdom that which is not destroyed" (Dan. 7:14, YLT). Again, *all* serve Him, not just *some*. That would be contradictory if the rebellious in hell contained the majority of His creation.

Paul summarized the end of all things in *I Corinthians*: "Now when all things are made subject to Him, then the Son Himself will also be subject to Him, who put all things under Him, that God may be all in all" (I Cor. 15:28). The righteousness of God through Christ realized in us is our salvation. Paul states here that God will one day be all in all of us, not all in some of us.

The theme of universal reconciliation recurs throughout the Bible. There are far too many verses that have to be rationalized away in order to hold to an infinite, unending torment paradigm. Here is a short list of Old Testament passages that unequivocally present the idea of universal reconciliation: Gen. 18:18; I Chr. 16:34; II Chr. 20:21: Job 42:2; Psa. 22:27, 106:1, 136; Isa. 9:7, 25:7-8, 40:5, 45:22-23, 53:5, 57:15-16; Eze. 18:4, 33:11; Lam. 3:22; Joel 2:28. Many more contain references to God's unending love and mercy.

In the New Testament the following passages present that same theme: Matt. 19:23-26; Luke 3:6; John 12:30; Acts 3:21; Rom. 5:18, 8:21-23, 11:15, 11:26, 11:32; I Cor. 15:22-28; II Cor. 5:19; Eph. 1:9-10; 1:22, 4:6, 4:9-10; Phi. 2:9-11; Col. 1:19, 2:13; I Tim. 2:3-4, 4:10; II Tim.:10; Tit. 2:11; Heb. 12:23; Jam. 1:18; I Pet. 3:19, 4:6; II Pet. 3:9, Rev. 4:11(w/

Eze. 18:23, 32). Each of these Scriptures is a direct reference to God's plan, ability, or desire to redeem all His creation—either in this realm or the next.

Those lists are not exhaustive. There are other references that some scholars interpret as being symbolic of God's plan to redeem all creation. Lists with over 600 Scriptural references on that theme have been published. However, we believe this list represents a compilation of the most unambiguous statements on universal reconciliation in Christ. So, in the words of George MacDonald, "Have courage! God will mend all!"

There is no escape from the Love that would have you righteous, peaceful and in joyous harmony with all of your brothers and sisters in Christ. This state can only be obtained through Divine connection. This connection can only be acquired through the free gift of resurrection life in Christ. It is the only solution to all pain and suffering. That is not to say we will not endure God's refining baptism of fire and discipline. The fire, and the outer darkness (for those outside of Christ's light) are not to be taken lightly, but they are remedial.

No man is without hope in this life or the next. We are all predestined to grow up to be like our Heavenly Father. Even the best of our childhood toys are designed to lose their magic as we mature. So too as we grow in Christ, we will require loftier spiritual realities to content us. As we pursue these higher longings, all suffering and injustice can and will be redeemed as spoken by all the prophets (Acts 3:21).

In conclusion, to assert there is no salvation after physical death and that all choice, which is the equivalent of freewill, is refused contradicts the Scriptural references in this book. It leaves reasonable questions about what happens to the souls of men who have died without ever knowing about Christ or hearing the gospel. Most importantly, it presents a contradictory and inconsistent message about the nature of God's love, wisdom and power.

The message of universal reconciliation in Christ answers the questions that many Christians have had to file away under "Check It Out Later". It is the consistent gospel message contained in all Scripture when seen in proper context.

Paul assures us that we can know what he told us is true because the very idea had to descend from something higher than our mere human knowledge. He wrote:

But as it is written: *"Eye has not seen, nor ear heard, nor have entered into the heart of man, the things, which God has prepared for those who love Him"*. But God has revealed them to us through His Spirit". (I Cor. 2:9, quoting Isa. 64:4).

That is good news! The bad news is, we all need to reconcile, so let's get started. Thy Kingdom Come!

Chapter 8

Answers:
To FAQs

While presenting the promise of universal reconciliation in Christ, some random questions inevitably fall outside the logical order of sequential chapters. Often this is because Scriptures are cited without considering the context in which they were written. Thus isolated verses are interpreted in a way not originally intended. This chapter will answer some of those **frequently asked questions** that have arisen. I would like to note that answers to these questions are in context with the Hebrew and Greek vocabulary defined in the earlier chapters. A sequential reading is recommended.

Q: What about the "blasphemy of the Holy Ghost", which is the unforgivable sin?

A: Jesus said, "Assuredly, I say to you, all sins will be forgiven the sons of men, and whatever blasphemies they may utter; but he who blasphemes against the Holy Spirit never has forgiveness, but is in danger of eternal condemnation—because they said, 'He has an unclean spirit'" (Mark 3:28-9, KJV). The NKJV translates it ...*is subject to eternal condemnation*. Most Bibles translate it, ...*is guilty of an eternal sin*. In all, eternal is an adjective defining the type of sin or condemnation.

Without any contextual clarification, this passage might appear to state that there is a limit to God's love. But what was the unforgivable sin Jesus was addressing, and why was it unforgivable?

Jesus had just been accused by Scribes from Jerusalem of using demonic powers to cast out demons (Mark 3:22). His reply to their charges was:

How can Satan cast out Satan? If a kingdom is divided against itself, that kingdom cannot stand. And if a house is divided against itself, that house cannot stand. And if Satan has risen up against himself, and is divided, he cannot stand, but has an end" (Mark 3:23-6).

Luke adds to the narrative spoken by Jesus, "If I cast out demons with the finger of God, surely the kingdom of God has come upon you" (Luke 11: 20).

The Scribes were accusing Jesus of using demonic powers or being a demon Himself. Thus they were ascribing the works of God to Satan, profaning the sacred. According to *Young's Analytical Concordance* the word *blaspheme* means to speak injuriously against. Crediting the spiritual truths and works of Christ to evil so as to prevent the needy from coming to Him would certainly be speaking injuriously. It is important to note that *blasphemes* is a present tense verb, and while people are committing such blasphemy, obviously they are rejecting God's kingdom. So any person, while they are rejecting Jesus as the Divine Word and Savior He claimed to be, is certainly in danger of eternal damnation. They are guilty of an eternal sin. However, does that mean God will not forgive a person who has blasphemed but later turns to Christ and repents?

The strength of the argument from those who believe there is a state of permanent *unforgiveness* revolves on the meaning of the words *never* and *eternal*. "He who blasphemes against the Holy Spirit never has forgiveness, but is in danger of eternal condemnation". As detailed in Chapter 2, the Greek words translated "never" would literally be rendered "not to the age", and "eternal" is literally "age-lasting". The concept that this sin, if repented of, would remain irreconcilable and unforgiven was not expressed. This is further clarified as the message goes on to say that a person who commits blasphemy against the Holy Spirit is "in danger" of eternal condemnation; that is not a *fait accompli*. So in context, that passage from *Mark* states that those who are rejecting the Holy Spirit in Jesus as the Divine authority, and are speaking out against Him, are in danger of age-lasting condemnation.

The only unforgivable sin is that of which the sinner will not repent, because that would condone the suffering sin ultimately perpetuates. As stated in the last chapter, the only requirement for forgiveness is confession and belief. The measurement of belief is of course action. Ask and it shall be given to you; seek and you will find.

Q: If all will be reconciled why did Jesus say only a few would find the path to life?
A: These are the words Christ spoke in context:

> Enter by the narrow gate; for wide *is* the gate and broad *is* the way that leads to destruction, and there are many who go in by it. Because narrow *is* the gate and difficult *is* the way which leads to life, and there are few who find it (Matt. 7:13-4).

If not given careful consideration, this passages can certainly sound like there is little or no hope for most of mankind. The way is "difficult" and few find it, at least in this life. In Noah's day only eight were saved. Yet Jesus, after His death, still preached the gospel to those lost in Noah's generation, so that they might "live according to God in the spirit". (See Ch. 3 pp 47-48). That would have been a pointless effort if physical death closed the door to eternal life.

So what is the pending destruction that most are headed for? This passage is the first of three references Christ makes near the end of the Sermon on the Mount regarding destruction. It is important to notice that contextual contrast lies between destruction and life, not perpetual suffering and life.

The second is about false prophets who will be known by their fruit, and the tree that bears bad fruit will be "cut down and thrown into the fire" (Matt. 7:15-20). Remember that trees are used as symbols for nations and kingdoms as well as people throughout Scripture. The 31st chapter in Ezekiel is a good example.

The third is the parable about a wise man who builds his house on the rock and a foolish man who builds on sand. "The winds blew and beat on that house [on the sand], and it fell" (Matt. 7:24-9). It is the house that is destroyed not the builder. The builder's work was ruined.

Back to the first statement of the wide straight path that leads to <u>destruction</u> and the difficult, narrow way that leads to life. The word describing those who enter the wide gate is not death (*thanatos*), but destruction (*apoleia*) which literally means separate, lose, and destroy. The root words of *apoleia* are *apo*, meaning separate, and *luo*, meaning lose or loose. *Strong's Concordance* describes *apollumi* (622, 684): "the idea is not extinction, but ruin, not of being, but of well-being". So what is being separated, lost or ruined? Their evil works are loosed and destroyed, thereby creating a state of well-being.

In the passage about the tree, it is the nation producing bad fruit as a result of the false prophets that is destroyed. In the parable about the foolish builder, it is his individual works. The difficult way is the way Christ taught us. "I am the <u>way</u>, the truth, and the life. No one comes to the Father except through Me." (John 14:6). As long as we are in the world, most people follow the way of the world. Not surprisingly, that is the broad and easy path of least resistance. It is the way of the world that will ultimately be separated from us and destroyed. Only a few will find the eternal life of Christ, in this world. The house of earthly gain and deception is on a foundation destined to be washed away. The only lasting structure is spiritual. The only secure foundation is built with the directives Christ gave us in His Sermon on the Mount.

Q: What about the "sin unto death"?

A: The *First Epistle of John* states, "…There is a sin unto death: I do not say that he should pray for it" (I John 5:16, KJV). Although John does not clarify what this sin is, looking at a passage from Jeremiah sheds some light on what is not to be prayed for. Jeremiah prophesied to the nation of Judah in the name of the Lord, "…And I spoke to you, rising up early and speaking, but you did not hear, and I called you, but you did not answer" (Jer. 7:13). The prophet then goes on to pronounce physical destruction, and "Therefore do not pray for this people, nor lift up a cry or prayer for them, nor make intercession to Me; for I will not hear you" (Jer. 7:16). Once again, the sin is non-repentance, and the punishment is physical death.

It is possible John may have been referring to the Zealots' refusal to recognize Jesus as the Christ. This rejection resulted in events that lead to the second destruction of the temple and the great dispersion in 70 A.D. foretold by Christ. Referencing the prophet Jeremiah and the historical parallel surrounding the destruction of the first temple would have driven the point home.

Regarding the matter of an unrepentant sinner in the Corinthian church, Paul states, "Deliver such a one to Satan for the destruction of the flesh, that his spirit may be saved…" (I Cor. 5:5). The consistent theme in these Scriptures is that of physical destruction for spiritual salvation. These Scriptures indicate the "sin unto death" is not a sin represented by a line that once crossed can never be redeemed. It is that sad state of non-repentance where the only means of salvation left is the door through physical death and into another realm of guidance.

Q: Will Judas be saved?

A: "Woe to that man by whom the Son of Man is betrayed! It would have been good for that man if he had not been born" (Matt. 26:24). This passage, referring to Judas, has been cited as a proof that not all will be saved. After all, how could it be good for Judas to never have been born if his birth assures he would one day be gathered into God's love forever?

First, to apply that interpretation to the passage creates a logical dilemma. It is unreasonable to relate good or bad to that which does not exist, such as would be the case if Judas had he not been born. So, stating that something would be good for a non-existent Judas would not make sense.

The literal translation reads, "It were good for him". The word "good" in that passage is a translation from the Greek word "*kalos*" which can also be translated "pleasing". The question is, how is it good for him? Is it good for him in an objective physical reality, which is illogical, or is it good in Judas' own opinion? Job, for a season, entertained the thought of his non-existence as pleasing, good or better for him: "May the day perish on which I was born" (Job 3:3). Judas' suffering over his betrayal caused him to regret his birth. He thought it good if he were not born as did Job. This interpretation creates a logical cohesive connection with the prediction of how the betrayal would affect the betrayer's reasoning and his consequential suicide.

Q: Will Hitler (or any other person responsible for genocide or mass murder) be saved?

A: If Scripture is to be believed, all will eventually be redeemed. That is not to say that horrific evil committed by people like Hitler will go unpunished. It may be a very long and painful road back to reconciliation (who knows?), but Scripture teaches that God is willing and able to, in the end, accomplish the salvation of all.

One would reasonably assume that those who are responsible for the agonizing deaths of millions of people would require a good deal more reconciliation than most. Their actions not only cut short the lives of those whose deaths they were directly responsible for, but also affected the lives of those who loved them and were connected to them. It is easy to imagine the reconciliation of such souls could take eons. But Scripture states ultimately all will be reconciled.

Eternal torment may seem to satisfy our personal desire for vengeance, but perhaps our own reconciliation process may soften our hearts for others.

Q: Will Satan be saved?
A: This is an interesting question. The way it is sometimes presented seems as if some prefer unending torment and suffering to reconciliation. The Scripture, as demonstrated throughout this book, states that all creation will be reconciled. The temporary suffering we are now experiencing is working for our benefit (II Cor. 4:17) much like the labor a woman experiences before the joy of receiving her child. Whatever damage Satan has caused, it must be recognized that he is a created being, and thus part of <u>all</u> creation being reconciled. It may serve us well to consider that much of his evil work needs our consensual assistance to accomplish. He may plant seeds of hatred, arrogance or whatever leads to suffering, but we are the ones who either nurture and act on, or uproot these thoughts. We have all contributed our share to the suffering of the world.

Referencing, yet again, the reconciliation of all created things in Christ, Paul writes:

> He is the image of the invisible God, the firstborn over all creation. For by Him <u>all</u> things were created that are in heaven and that are on earth, visible and invisible, whether thrones or dominions or principalities or powers. <u>All</u> things were created through Him and for Him. And He is before all things, and in Him <u>all</u> things consist. And He is the head of the body, the church, who is the beginning, the firstborn from the dead, that in <u>all</u> things He may have the preeminence. For it pleased *the Father that* in Him all the fullness should dwell and by Him to reconcile <u>all</u> things to Himself, by Him, whether things on earth or things in heaven, having made peace through the blood of His cross (Col 1:15-20).

So the <u>all</u> of the created things is the same <u>all</u> that will be reconciled. It is clearly in the same context of thought. All things were created through Him and for Him, and will be reconciled to Him by Him. Satan's evil can only sub-serve an all-wise God for an eternal good that is promised to be realized one day. John writes of that day in *Revelation*:

> And every creature which is in heaven and on the earth and under the earth and such as are in the sea, and all that are in them, I heard saying:
> "Blessing and honor and glory and power
> *Be* to Him who sits on the throne,
> And to the Lamb, forever and ever!" (Rev. 5:13)

Here it appears that every creature in creation is worshiping God. "For of Him and through Him and to Him *are* all things, to whom *be* glory forever. Amen." (Rom. 11:36)

Q: "You are of *your* father the devil" (John 8:39). Doesn't this statement by Jesus prove we are not all children of God and that God is not a Father to all?

A: *Genesis* clearly states, "So God created man in His *own* image; in the image of God He created him; male and female He created them" (Gen. 1:27). That makes us all the offspring of God. This parentage cannot be abdicated. So in what sense are some children of the devil? It is in the nature of identifying behavior. Behavior can be renounced. What parent hasn't at one time or another said in jest to the other parent, that is your child not mine; and moments later claim that's my boy or girl? Jesus, of course, was not jesting. But the same point was well made in the context as it was referencing the attitudes and behaviors of those to whom He was speaking. He wanted to drive home the point that a true child is one in spirit with his or her parents. Jesus said, "If you were Abraham's children, you would do the works of Abraham" (John 8:39).

Q: Paul said God's ways are "past finding out" (Rom. 11:33). So, what can we know about God?

A: In that passage from Romans, Paul was referencing his previous statement that God, having committed all to disobedience, would have mercy on all. God's ways truly are past our ability to discover. Thus they must be revealed to us. So what is God's way that is past our ability to comprehend? In the context of that passage, it is the concept that the desire, wisdom and ability of God is to save <u>all</u>. Most people want criminals to be punished, but God wants people to repent and be restored. Punishment may help accomplish that end, but for the satisfaction of revenge, men frequently do not want evildoers to repent. This was the case with Jonah.

When God asked Jonah to "cry out against" the wickedness of the people of Nineveh, Jonah tried to flee. The Assyrian Empire, whose capital city was Nineveh, was legendary for its tyranny and brutality. Ninevite kings bragged about stacking the corpses or heads of their enemies at the gates of their conquered cities. Nahum prophesied against Nineveh, "Woe to the bloody city. It *is* all full of lies and robbery…—because of the multitude of harlotries of the seductive harlot, the mistress of sorceries" (Nah. 3:1, 4). The culture of Nineveh centered on the cultic worship of Ishtar, the goddess of sexual love and war.

No wonder Jonah wanted to flee. However, God sent a storm, and Jonah was cast overboard, swallowed by a fish, and spit out on the shore. So Jonah went back and preached to the Ninevites. An interesting side note is that there is indication of the city also worshipping Dagon, the Philistine's half fish half man idol. Imagine how disturbing a man vomited out by a fish on their shore must have been to that culture.

> Then God saw their works, that they turned from their evil ways; and God relented from the disaster that He had said He would bring upon them, and He did not do it. But it displeased Jonah exceedingly, and he became angry. So he prayed to the LORD, and said: "Ah, LORD, was not

this what I said when I was still in my country? Therefore I fled previously to Tarshish; for I know that You *are* a gracious and merciful God, slow to anger and abundant in loving kindness, One who relents from doing harm" (Jon. 3:10 – 4:1-2).

As was the case with the Ninevites, the "ways past finding out" Paul referred to was God's *mercy*, His propensity to forgive even the worst of people who repent. Jonah thought the Ninevites were unworthy of mercy. However, God's view was more encompassing. "And should I not pity Nineveh, that great city, in which are more than one hundred and twenty thousand persons who cannot discern between their right hand and the left..." (Jon. 4:11). Such compassion may often go against our human nature that wants wrongdoers to suffer. But God desires enlightenment, repentance and reconciliation.

Q: Since God's ways are higher than ours, who are you to question God or Divine retribution?
A: The inquiry "Who are you to question God?" usually means, "Who are you to question my interpretation of scripture?" Honesty and purity require the responsible questioning of concepts, especially if they seem dark.

Jesus asked, "Yes, and why, even of yourselves, do you not judge what is right?" (Luke 12:57). Asking us to make such judgments would be a mockery if we lacked the capacity to do so.

Those who believe Scriptures teach unending torment often justify that belief by citing references that the mind of God is unknowable. They may quote the Apostle Paul, "Oh the depth of the riches both of the wisdom and knowledge of God! How unsearchable *are* His judgments, and His ways past finding out" (Rom. 11:33). The prophet Isaiah presented the same idea, "For as the heavens are higher than the earth, so are My ways higher than your ways, and My thoughts than your thoughts" (Isa. 55:9).

The verses immediately preceding those passages reveal the inscrutable ways of God are His mercy and His forgiveness of sin—not His condemnation of mankind. "For God hath concluded them all in unbelief that He might have mercy upon all" (Rom. 11:32). There the real mystery is unveiled. God's mercy upon all is that which is far beyond our comprehension, not His wrath. Everyone has been lost in unbelief in order that God might have mercy on everyone.

Likewise, the verse immediately preceding Isaiah 55:9 ("My ways are not your ways") states, "Let the wicked forsake his way, and the unrighteous man his thoughts; let him return to the Lord. And He will have mercy on him; and our God, for He will abundantly pardon" (Isa. 55:7). The incomprehensible mystery of God is not that He condemns people to unending torment, but that with only the forsaking of unrighteousness, He forgives the repentant. Both of these Scriptures about God's ways being far above our ways are referring to God's propensity to pardon and to execute mercy.

Q: If "It is appointed for men to die once, but after this the judgment", what hope can remain after that?

A: Jesus said, "For judgment I have come into this world that those who do not see may see and those who see may be made blind" (John 9:39). In another place He said, "If therefore the light that is in thee be darkness, how great is that darkness!" (Matt. 6:23). To judge means to discern between right and wrong, truth and lies, light and darkness.

As explained in Chapter 1, punishment is not justice. Sentencing and punishment come after a verdict or judgment. Christ came to reveal truth to those who do not know, but desire truth and to expose the lies of those who claim to know truth but act against it. Jesus clarified that declaration when He said:

> I have come as a light into the world, that whoever believes in Me should not abide in darkness. And if anyone hears my words and does not believe, I do not

judge him; for I did not come to judge the world but to save the world" (John 12:46-7).

So Christ came for judgment but not to judge. How does that make sense?

The world is already condemned. "And this is the condemnation, that the light has come into the world, and men loved darkness rather than light, because their deeds were evil" (John 3:19). We are already condemned to the consequences of our bad choices, or poor judgments. Consider the condition of the world.

Jesus came for judgment (discerning revelation) not to judge (condemn). The chaos in the world's political systems testifies against man's standard of judgment. The passage in Hebrews 9:27, states that judgment (discerning revelation) comes after death. The judgment and understanding of our own choices in the burning light of truth may save us. But many may continue to condemn themselves to the consequences of evil by rejecting the Word of God. Most importantly, the world is in a state of ongoing judgments and Scripture speaks of more than one judgment after death. Clearly the judgment at our death is not the final judgment. The English poet William Blake thought of it in this sense, "Whenever any Individual Rejects Error & Embraces Truth, a Last Judgment passes upon that Individual" (*Poems and Prophecies*, 366).

Q: What about God's wrathful punishments? Doesn't God's wrath prove He is not always loving?

A: "For I will not contend forever, nor will I always be angry; for the spirit would fail before Me, and the souls which I have made" (Isa. 57:16). Parents are sometimes angry with their children. Why? Given emotionally healthy parents, anger is usually provoked because a child is behaving in a manner that is destructive to themselves or others. Punishment is intended for correction, and to correct a child properly is to show love for the child. It is motivated by a desire to help the child become a better person. What stable, wise, loving parent would destroy or forever abandon their offspring? Is God any less loving?

In *Romans*, Paul talks about some who are consistently resistant to the call of God because they prefer to believe their own illusions and imaginings. The letter states that the wrath of God is revealed from heaven against them. How? He gave them over to the consequences of their behavior. If intervention stopped all perverse desire and action, no one would learn to discern good from evil and choice would not exist.

The purpose of the wrath of God is to destroy sin, not the souls which God made. It is motivated by love. God has chosen to have individual souls be the slayers of evil in themselves through the knowledge of its destructive nature and the receiving of Divine empowerment. Paul wrote:

> For the wrath of God is revealed from heaven against all ungodliness and unrighteousness of men, who suppress the truth in unrighteousness, because what may be known of God is manifest in them, for God has shown *it* to them" (Rom. 1:18-9).

This Scripture implies that, in some sense, we are being judged now.

In fact, there are over four hundred Scriptures referencing judgments, most of which occur in this life. Paul wrote to Timothy, "Some men's sins are clearly evident, preceding *them* to judgment, but those of some *men* follow later. Likewise, the good works *of some* are clearly evident, and those that are otherwise cannot be hidden" (I Tim. 5:24-5). Some men's sins are open beforehand, going before to judgment. Some judgments follow after. Judgment is constantly going on.

Even the "Great White Throne" judgment is not called the "last judgment" in scripture. Some have assumed it the last, because it is the last recorded judgment.

Q: What about the separation of the sheep and the goats in Matthew 25? Did not Jesus teach that the sheep would inherit the kingdom prepared for them and the goats would depart into the everlasting fire prepared for the devil and his angels?

A: Christ gave us the timing of that event: "When the Son of Man comes in His glory" (Matt. 25:31). He had previously explained that it would occur before the death of some of those standing in His presence at that time. "For the Son of Man will come in the glory of His Father with His angels, and then He will reward each according to his works. Assuredly, I say to you there are some standing here who shall not taste death till they see the Son of Man coming in His glory (Matt. 16:27-8).

The context of Christ's narrative reveals the sheep and goats represent nations. "All the nations will be gathered before Him, and He will separate them…" (Matt. 25:32). The word translated nations is *ethnos*, which literally means groups or communities of people. So the separation is not referencing individual people, but groups. But why use sheep and goats as analogies? As Christ often did, He was referring to Old Testament Scripture. Jeremiah wrote: "…go forth out of the land of the Chaldeans and be as the he goats before the flocks" (Jer. 50:8, KJV). The goats represent community leaders. Zechariah wrote, "I punished the goats" (Zech. 10:3), for leading the flock astray.

So, given the timing of the events and identity of the goats, a logical explanation of Christ's statement would be that He was prophesying 70 A.D. events in Jerusalem, some forty years hence. Those were the last days of the Old Testament age, for that is when the temple and its sacrificial system was destroyed. Only those who obeyed the warning of Jesus to flee the city immediately escaped (Matt. 24:16-8). The temple priests and zealots were killed. That destruction ended once and for all the Old Testament age and ushered in the New Testament age where Christ alone is the high priest.

Now, the only acceptable sacrifices are spiritual and offered through Him. (For a more complete explanation of 70 A.D. events read Josephus's *War of the Jews*.)

Q: Are we capable of understanding Divine justice?

A: God commands us to make moral judgments. If our sense of justice differs from His, then all morality would be relative—and thus pointless. Moral relativism would render describing God as "good" meaningless, because what we might mean by good may be evil to God. Since morality means an adherence to principles of right and wrong, there must be a standard by which to judge. God himself has given us His standard through Christ.

Jesus rebuked men for not judging what was right. The doctrinal positions of the Pharisees were skewed as a result of ignoring their own conscience. They ignored the law of love in favor of the legalistic letter of the law and skewed the character of God whenever the two came into conflict. For example, the Pharisees condemned Jesus for healing (working) on the Sabbath (John 7:23-4). He admonished them to judge righteously implying they had the capacity to do so.

The Old Testament is replete with Scriptures about man's responsibility to judge and to do what is right. Here are some examples:

- You shall do no injustice in judgment. You shall not be partial to the poor, nor honor the person of the mighty. In righteousness you shall judge your neighbor (Lev. 19:15).
- Then I commanded your judges at that time, saying "Hear *the cases* between your brethren, and judge righteously between a man and his brother or the stranger who is with him" (Deut. 1:16).
- Therefore give to your servant an understanding heart to judge your people, that I may discern between good and evil (I Kings 3:9).

The last quote is a prayer of Solomon, referring to himself as God's "servant". These commandments to judge fairly imply that people are fully capable of discerning what is just.

Q: Why haven't I heard this before?
A: This doctrine is certainly not new. It was the common belief of the early church for several centuries, and is part of Eastern Orthodoxy today. The Puritans brought with them the current Western doctrinal paradigms. (See Chapter 5 on Anselm and Abelard for a brief history.) Denominational teachings are often filtered through presuppositions.

Thus, Scripture is often studied in fragments supporting a particular paradigm. Assumptions lend themselves to quick and unexamined readings, especially when one is not exposed to other possible interpretations or is not familiar with all Scripture. When those filters are removed and passages are read in their entire context, there is a greater freedom to hear what the writers of Scripture intended.

God's message of universal redemption appears in almost every book of the New Testament. It shines through quite brightly, if it is not filtered out. The Western Latinized Church adopted Anselm's legal paradigm near the turn of the millennium while Eastern Orthodoxy rejected it. Lack of exposure to various opinions can create tunnel vision.

Q: Could people arrive at the concept of universal reconciliation by reading the Scriptures on their own?
A: History certainly says yes. Most people in the early church believed it, and it was the prevalent theological position for the first few centuries. Because it is the most cohesive interpretation, it took centuries of theological and political wrangling to remove that message. Nevertheless, the universal reconciliation paradigm remains held by some in nearly all Christian denominations around the world. This eschatology has withstood both the test of time and many denominational attempts to eradicate it.

Perhaps the question should be posed another way. Would most people arrive at some common contemporary doctrines by studying Scripture on their own? My husband related a story to me about a Christian friend of his during the first years of his Christian walk. He had taken a job working the graveyard shift at a gas station. Since he had a lot of quiet time on his hands, he read the Bible through, cover to cover. He commented that he would never have come up with some of the doctrine being taught in church from just reading the Word.

Q: Are there any other prominent Christian thinkers who have written about the possibility of salvation after death and/or universal reconciliation in Christ?

A: Martin Luther wrote a letter to Hanseu Von Rechenberg in 1522 on the "question of whether or not God may or will save those who die without faith." In it Luther said, "God forbid that I should limit the time of acquiring faith to the present life. In the depth of the Divine mercy there may be opportunity to win it in the future" (cited in *The Salvation of All*, Pilkington, 293).

C.S. Lewis is perhaps the most popular Christian writer of all time. His novel *The Great Divorce* was one of the first steps on my spiritual journey. It is about the split between heaven and hell, where several souls take a trip from hell (or purgatory) to the outskirts of heaven. Throughout the book Lewis describes the development of some ghostly souls into real people able to withstand the solidness of heaven. But even though some decide to stay, many choose to return to their dark insubstantial world. Lewis seems to differ with his mentor George MacDonald on that point.

I see heaven as a much more irresistible realm than Lewis did. Not that the process of reconciliation is not work, but it is work we will all eventually desire to do. We are not designed to live in isolation. Darkness eventually makes us long for light. I cannot imagine anyone forever pursuing a self-absorbed vicarious state once they have glimpsed the reality of

God's love. If there is the possibility of choosing to live in light or darkness after death, as presented in *The Great Divorce*, the logical extension of that premise is that all will ultimately choose light. Scripture consistently reveals that message.

Watchman Nee was the founder of the *local church* in China, a growing network of small home churches that exist with the state-sponsored church. He wrote several popular books over about a 30-year period. In 1956 he was imprisoned on trumped-up charges by the communist government. He died in a labor camp, leaving a shakily written note under his pillow that ended, "I die because of my belief in Christ". In his book *God's Plan and the Overcomers* Nee wrote:

God created all things and mankind for the sake of manifesting His glory. Today, believers are manifesting a little something of Christ. But one day, all things shall manifest Christ because the whole universe shall be filled with Him. In creating all things, God desires that all things will manifest Christ (5).

Oswald Chambers is the author of the classic Christian daily devotional *My Utmost for His Highest*. He wrote:

It is an injustice to say that Jesus Christ labored in redemption to make me a saint. Jesus Christ labored in redemption to redeem the whole world and to place it perfectly whole and restored before the throne of God (Feb 1).

Reconciliation means the restoring of the relationship between the entire human race and God, putting it back to what God designed it to be (July 12).

There are several websites listing hundreds of famous people who believed in universal reconciliation. The list is much too long to include here, but most lists begin by referencing almost all the early church fathers. A few readily recognized authors include: Nathaniel Hawthorne, Hans Christian Andersen, Henry Wadsworth Longfellow, Alfred Lord Tennyson, William Makepiece Thackery, Charles Dickens, Lewis Carroll, Walt Whitman, Henry James, Robert Bulwer Lytton, James Fenimore Cooper, Victor Hugo, William Morris, Bret Harte, Hannah Whitehall Smith, Charles M. Schultz, Madelyn L'Engle, and many, many more.

Q: Did Jesus ever reference universal reconciliation?
A: Jesus said, "To what shall I liken the Kingdom of God. It is like leaven, which a woman took and hid in three measures of meal, till the <u>whole</u> was leavened" (Luke 13:20-1). The church is often taught that leaven is a symbol for sin or false doctrine because of Christ's reference to the "leaven of the Pharisees" (Matt. 16:6-12). But leaven is simply used as an agent causing change, either lies or truth.

Q: If God will save all, what is there to fear?
A: It is the nature of Love in God that needs to be feared, because He will not leave you to continue forever in destructive ways. God will do whatever is necessary to help you understand and repent of the evil that is killing you and harming others—because He loves you. The fact that He will not abandon you should either bring you comfort or fear.

Jesus revealed that God is a loving Father, always looking after our welfare. A king may abdicate his crown, but a father is a father forever. God is not our loving Abba Father at one moment and our threatening Mafia Godfather the next. God's wrath is not for self-gratification but for our benefit. Jesus said, "He who has seen me has seen the Father" (John 14:9). If we believe those words, we should be careful about attributing to the Father what we have not seen in the Son.

Q: If everyone will eventually get saved, why bother with the great commission? What is the point of evangelism?

A: To be saved is to love and be reconciled with all. Love is the motivating factor. The sooner we are reconciled the better. The further one moves away from wholeness and unity with God and His creation, the more difficult the process of getting back to restoration. To know God is to be part of this gathering commission. It is the desire to have God's Kingdom come into the hearts of all men. Helping others to live a more significant and abundant life is food for the soul. "Through one man sin entered the world, and death through sin, and thus death spread to all men, because all sinned" (Rom. 5:12). It will take the deliverance of all to rid the universe of evil. If "the last enemy *that* will be destroyed *is* death" (I Cor. 15:26), it follows that sin, the cause of death, will also be eradicated.

Many people mistakenly believe universal reconciliation implies there is no hell, since the outcome for all is the same. However, nothing could be further from the truth. Scripture is clear that there is an unseen state of suffering in which people will experience the purging of unrepentant sin. But we do not believe it is a permanent condition for anyone. Since eternal life is to know God (John 17:3), and God is present even "if I make my bed in Hades" (Psa. 139:8), He can reach out to us with love and truth even there.

As for me, the knowledge that all will one day be reconciled in Christ elevates everyone to the status of a person with whom I will share eternity, regardless of our current relationship or circumstances. I am in awe, when I consider that they, along with me, will one day be conformed into the image of Christ. How can I not want to hurry that along?

The Great Commission is to spread the good news of the Kingdom of God and salvation from sin. "The notion that the salvation of Jesus is a salvation from the consequences of our sins, is a false, mean, low notion. The salvation of Christ is salvation from the smallest tendency or leaning to sin" (MacDonald, *Creation*, 75-6). "Go ye therefore, and teach all nations, baptizing them in the name of the Father, and of the Son, and of the Holy Ghost: Teaching them to observe all things whatsoever I have commanded you" (Matt. 28:20).

Bibliography

Ballou, Hosea. *The Ancient History of Universalism* (Providence, RI: Z. Baker, 1842).

Barclay, William. *New Testament Words* (Louisville, KT: Westminster John Knox Press, 2000).

Barclay, William. *A Spiritual Autobiography* (Grand Rapids, MI: William B. Eerdmans Publishing, 1975).

Beauchemin, Gerry. *Hope Beyond Hell* (Olmito, TX: Malista Press, 2007).

Blake, William. *Poems and Prophecies* (New York: Alfred A Knopf, 1991).

Chambers, Oswald. *My Utmost for His Highest*, ed. James Reimann, Updated Edition. (Grand Rapids, MI: Discovery House Publishers, 1992).

Clemens, Titus Falvius (aka St. Clement of Alexandria). *St. Clement of Alexandra Selected Works: Excerpted from The Ante-Nicene Fathers Translations of The Writings of the Fathers down to a.d. 325*. ed. Paul A. Böer, Sr. (Veritas Splendor Publications, 2012).

Edwards, Jonathan. *Sinners in the Hands of an Angry God*. www.ccel.org/ccel/edwards/sermons.sinners.html.

Hanson, John Wesley, D.D. *Bible Proofs of Universal Salvation* (Chicago, 1877, reprinted by A.W. Hall).

Hanson, John Wesley, D.D. *Universalism, the Prevailing Doctrine of the Christian Church During Its First Five Hundred Years* (BibioBazaar, 1899).

Holy Bible, New King James Version. (Nashville, TN: Thomas Nelson Publishers, 1994).

Hurley, Loyal F. *The Outcome of Infinite Grace.* (Santa Clarita, CA: Concordant Publishing Concern)

Kalomiros, Dr. Alexandre. "The River of Fire". (Seattle, WA: St. Nectarios Press, 1980) A reprint of a presentation at the 1980 Orthodox Conference in Seattle, WA. www.orthodoxpress.org/parish/river_of_fire.htm.

Lewis, C.S. *The Abolition of Man* (New York: HarperCollins, 2001).

Lewis, C.S. *The Great Divorce* (New York: Touchstone, 1996).

Lewis, C.S. *Mere Christianity* (New York: HarperCollins, 1980).

MacDonald, George. *Creation in Christ*, ed. Rolland Hein (Wheaton, IL: Harold Shaw Publishers, 1978).

MacDonald, George. *Unspoken Sermons Series I, II, III* (Whitehorn, CA: Johannesen, 1999).

Nee, Watchman. *God's Plan and the Overcomers* (Christian Literature Crusade: 1980).

Parry, Robin A. and Partridge, Christopher H. eds. *Universal Salvation? The Current Debate* (Grand Rapids, MI: William B. Eerdmans Publishing, 2003).

Pilkington, Clyde L. Jr. *The Salvation of All* (Windber, PA: Bible Student's Press, 2010).

Sheen, Fulton J. *The Choice: The Sacred or Profane Life* (New York: Dell Publishing, 1963).

Sittser, Gerald L. *Water from a Deep Well* (Downers Grove, IL: InterVarsity, 2007).

Stetson, Eric. *Christian Universalism* (Sparkling Bay Books, 2008).

Strong, James. *The New Strong's Expanded Exhaustive Concordance of the Bible* (Nashville, TN: Thomas Nelson, 2010).

Talbott, Thomas. *The Inescapable Love of God* (Universal Publishers, 1999).

Thompson, Francis. *Complete Poems of Francis Thompson* (First Rate Publishers, 2015).

Yamaguchi, Miho, PhD. *George MacDonald's Challenging Theology of the Atonement, Suffering, and Death* (Tucson, AZ: Wheatmark, 2007).

Young, Robert. *Young's Literal Translation of the Holy Bible.* (Benediction Classics, 2012).

Index

www.ingramcontent.com/pod-product-compliance
Lightning Source LLC
LaVergne TN
LVHW091258080426
835510LV00007B/313